Oskar Schlemmer
Man

Teaching notes from the Bauhaus

Edited by Heimo Kuchling

Translated by Janet Seligman

The M.I.T. Press

Cambridge, Massachusetts

Originally published by Florian Kupferberg,
Mainz and Berlin, under the title "Der Mensch"

English translation
Copyright © 1971 by
The Massachusetts Institute of Technology
and Lund Humphries Publishers Limited

Printed and bound in Great Britain by
Lund Humphries, Bradford and London

ISBN 0 262 19095 8 (hard cover)

Library of Congress catalog card number : 72–151722

Contents

,

Preface	6
Editor's note	7
Introduction	9
Oskar Schlemmer's conception of man	23
Syllabuses – Teaching schedules	25
Drawing from the nude	41
Measurement and proportion	55
Natural sciences	71
Figure drawing	79
Linear figures	85
Plane and spatial schemata	97
The moving figure	113
The figure in space	124
Stylistic analyses	127
Philosophy	130
Psychology	143
Questions and answers to the preliminary course 'man'	148
Postscript	152

Preface

Oskar Schlemmer has hitherto figured in this series [of Bauhaus books] only as co-author of a book entitled *Die Bühne im Bauhaus*. Another publication, called *Bühnenelemente*, appeared in the prospectus of the Bauhausbücher of the 1920's but was never issued; publishing opportunities dwindled around 1929–30 in proportion as economic stagnation and political oppression increased. It is largely the initiative and sympathetic co-operation of Mrs Tut Schlemmer that have made it possible for the notes for his classes of 1928 and 1929 left by Oskar Schlemmer at his death to appear here. All who have drawn upon Schlemmer's papers and have been intellectually enriched by so doing are, as we are, indebted to Mrs Schlemmer, who preserved them and made them available.

Its origin alone makes this book naturally suited to form part of the Bauhaus series. As we can see most clearly today, Schlemmer's intellectual ideas coincided with those of the Bauhaus to an extent which otherwise only those of Gropius himself and of Moholy did – in a different way. However important for the Bauhaus the problems raised by technology and their solution may have been – the goal, to which all else was, and continued to be, subordinated, was man the social animal, and, all social engagement notwithstanding, the individual.

The publication and editing of this book has been a difficult task, because Schlemmer left the material in the form of unsorted notes. The writer believes, with Mrs Tut Schlemmer, that he has found in Heimo Kuchling a collaborator excellently equipped for the job. His professional qualification rests upon the many years he has spent as editor of *Kontur*, a journal devoted to aesthetic questions, and on the teaching staffs of both the Akademie der bildenden Künste, and (recently) the master classes for sculpture in Vienna.

Hans M. Wingler

Editor's note

Oskar Schlemmer was unable to publish his Bauhaus course on 'man' himself. He was not entrusted with that department until the early part of 1928 – and in October 1929 his departure from the Bauhaus was solemnized. So short a period of teaching gave Schlemmer no time to elaborate the material of his classes in the light of practical experience and to work it up into a book. It is a framework, a broadly sketched plan, the centre of which is undoubtedly the section on figure drawing. This section is also the most personal; in it Schlemmer has set down his own experiences of shaping a human figure.

There is no clue as to which of the over two hundred sheets Schlemmer himself would have selected, nor how he would have put the material together and amplified it to make a book. The sheets are only sporadically dated and numbered. Some of them carry a note of the day of the class. But the dating is not continuous either and is therefore no guide. The teaching material in the schedules of work is arranged in parallel subjects, so that there is no hard and fast order here, especially as notes do not exist to support all the material proposed in the schedules.

In contrast to the Bauhaus books which have already appeared, the material which constitutes the plan for this book is not restricted to purely formal problems and its author's subjective ideas. Many of Schlemmer's notes are excerpts from works on the natural sciences, psychology and philosophy; even the chapter on the teaching of measurement and proportion consists largely of borrowed material. Had this chapter been printed in full, it would have overweighted the book with familiar, impersonal material. We have therefore included only those parts of the groundwork for the classes which are Schlemmer's own or which illustrate the syllabus for the scientific subjects. Where it seemed important, the tables drawn up by Schlemmer for his teaching have been included. The contents of the material in question are given in the introductory paragraphs with which each section begins. The works cited are taken from a bibliography compiled by Schlemmer himself. In order to strengthen the personal note of the book, the section on drawing from the nude has been made to include some of Schlemmer's own drawings of the nude figure. And since the roots of his teaching of figure drawing lie in Schlemmer's own form, we have reproduced in the appendix a few drawings by the Bauhaus master which provide an insight into the development of his formal vocabulary.

Some responses to this preliminary course emerge from the students' answers to questions set by Schlemmer.

The existing notes provide an incomplete picture of Schlemmer's personality as a teacher and we have therefore supplemented this picture in the introduction and, where possible, in the texts of the introductory paragraphs, with passages from diaries and letters in which Schlemmer discusses the Bauhaus and his teaching or questions of artistic form.

The page numbers of the passages from Oskar Schlemmer's diary and letters refer to the book, *Oskar Schlemmer, Briefe und Tagebücher*, published by Albert Langen – Georg Müller, Munich, 1958.

My thanks go first and foremost to Mrs Tut Schlemmer, who not only preserved the material, had it photocopied, and put it into preliminary order, but also assisted the editorial work by word and deed. I thank also my friends Erich Ess and Peter Pichl for the trouble they have taken in reading proofs and my wife for her help in transcribing Schlemmer's holograph texts. And finally I thank the Deutsche Bücherei in Leipzig for having supplied the bibliographical information.

Heimo Kuchling

Introduction

'No sooner had the visitor been led across the next border, than
he noticed an entirely different manner of building. The houses
were no longer scattered, they no longer resembled huts; they
were instead regularly grouped, large and handsome outside,
spacious, comfortable and elegant within; here was an un-
restricted, well-built town, well adapted to the surroundings.
The fine arts and their related crafts are at home here and a quite
unusual silence reigns over these places.

'Our traveller was struck by the gravity, the wonderful austerity
with which both beginners and the more advanced were treated;
it seemed as though nothing were done out of a man's own
power and mastery but as though everyone were animated
through and through, by a secret spirit, leading towards one
great goal. Nowhere was there a draft or sketch, every line was
drawn with deliberation, and when the traveller asked the guide
to explain the whole procedure, he said that imaginative power
is anyhow a vague, uncertain faculty, whereas the whole merit
of the creative artist consists in his learning to define and fix it
ever more closely and finally indeed to raise it into a presence.

'He was reminded of the necessity for firm foundations in other
arts. Would a musician permit his pupil to run his fingers wildly
over the strings or to invent intervals according to his own choice
and inclination? It is obvious here that nothing is to be left to the
whim of the learner; the element in which he is to work is deci-
sively stated; the tool he is to use is placed in his hand, even the
way and manner in which he is to use it . . .

'In other places . . . display may prove necessary, but not with us.
Our whole nature and existence is display. You see here buildings
of all kinds, all executed by pupils; admittedly from designs which
have been discussed and thought out a hundred times: for the
builder must not grope about and experiment; that which is to

remain standing must stand properly and must suffice, if not for eternity, yet for a long time. Though we may continually make mistakes, we must not build any.'[1]

[1] Johann Wolfgang Goethe, *Wilhelm Meister's Travels*, Book 2, *'The Man Aged Fifty Years'*, chapter 8.

In Goethe's vision, quoted by Oskar Schlemmer in the notes to his 'Course on man', the Bauhaus master saw the ideal of the Bauhaus: it should be a centre of work and teaching with a conscious goal, co-ordinating the arts and examining the laws of form, a refuge for artistic reflection, in which new ideas would be born and tested and in which they could mature. Harmonious collaboration between teachers and pupils was to create a total work of art combining architecture, painting, and sculpture, which was to set the path for the future and clarify the confusion of period styles.

Reality allowed but a fragment of the large ideal to come to fruition. It could not have been otherwise. Yet the quality and the spirit of the Bauhaus were so strong and new that the Bauhaus is still regarded as the model for institutions of art education, and not without justification. The topical interest of the Bauhaus makes it incumbent upon the editor of notes for a Bauhaus book left unprepared at the author's death to draw attention to the problems of this teaching establishment as Schlemmer saw them; for only thus can we gain a complete insight into the manner in which Schlemmer conceived his book. Oskar Schlemmer was, as we see today, the teacher at the Bauhaus who had the Bauhaus idea as a whole most clearly in view and who was also continually striving to see its central artistic aspiration – the union of the arts in architectonic work – realized. Though the Bauhaus fell short of its theory both as a totality and in detail, Schlemmer tried to achieve it within his own subject.

It is clear, simply from how much of the Bauhaus idea these Bauhaus books by the painters of the institution do and do not contain, which problems were soluble and which insoluble, which parts of the artistic programme of the Bauhaus could be completely, which fragmentarily, realized and which could not be realized at all.

The problems which the Bauhaus painters saw confronting them as teachers were complex and exceedingly difficult to solve. No matter from which angle it is viewed, art is unteachable. Only a certain repertoire of forms can be passed on and taught, but this does not become a work of art unless it is intellectually grounded and creatively applied. The founders of the Bauhaus were aware of the shortcomings of academic theories and endeavoured to eradicate them. It was for the time and for the personality of the teachers to provide the intellectual foundation for the teaching. Art education was to be built afresh on a foundation of crafts and with the aid of the 'pure' creative means which the pioneer artists of the period had discovered. Thus artists concerned with the analysis of creative means as well as first-rate craftsmen were appointed to be teachers at the Bauhaus.

The intellectual foundation which the time and their company offered to the Bauhaus was neither rigid nor homogeneous. Although the idea that during the great European stylistic periods the intellectual world had been homogeneous has long ceased to be tenable, it is nevertheless certain that the fundamental relationships of man with man, the world and God were not questioned in principle at these periods and that there were indeed consistent theories of life — even if several often existed concurrently. Theories of life of this kind continued into the last century — for example, the mechanistic and the vitalistic. It was not until the twentieth century that the endeavour to create a theory of life was abandoned; instead, all that concerns man's relationship with his world and with himself was called into question.

The theory of life was replaced in the best instances by a postulation of antagonisms which influence the life of men and art. Schlemmer recognized two great opposites: 'The sign of our times is . . . mechanization, the inexorable process which takes possession of every sphere of life and art. Everything which can be mechanized is being mechanized. Result: we recognize what is unmechanizable.'[2] The mechanizable and unmechanizable are poles between which the life and work of modern man is played out. The postulation of such antagonisms is an idea which may still be capable of fertilizing art, for the artist sees himself in an intellectual field of force from which he receives impulses for creation. Yet Schlemmer sensed the inadequacy and poverty of such ideas and he lectured to his audience on the history of philosophy in order to find firm intellectual ground.

'We the modern moderns!' was the battle-cry of the *Bauhäusler*. This battle-cry included both an attack on the outmoded academies and a programme for their own teaching. At the Bauhaus 'being modern' did not mean giving free reign to whim; on the contrary, it meant anchoring creative art in craftsmanship and seeing in architecture the centre to which the arts and crafts should relate. The academies cultivated the 'free arts', which had no coherence in themselves and were not related to one another. The academies shunned the crafts and were proud of the fact that they had no connexion with them.

In order to gain a better understanding of the programme, problems, and influence of the Bauhaus, we must glance at the working of the academies of the time, which the Bauhaus deliberately opposed.

The latest repertoire of forms available to the academies to hand down and teach was the neo-classical. The basic problem to emerge from this repertoire concerned the relationship between form and content: the form was drawn from the remote past, the

[2] *Die Bühne im Bauhaus. Oskar Schlemmer, Mensch und Kunstfigur.* Neue Bauhausbücher. Florian Kupferberg (Mainz and Berlin, 1965).

content was moulded by the intellectual currents of the time. The split between form and content made the intellectual ground on which the academies stood precarious and questionable. Since, however, the neo-classical formal repertoire had a historically distinct, assessable and measurable model, neo-classicism became the embodiment of academicism. Only when the naturalistic components of neo-classicism undermined and finally ousted the idealistic was the rigid formal scheme dissolved and superseded by 'drawing' and 'painting' from the model; all that remained of the neo-classical formal scheme was 'composition', which as an idealistic scheme of order was forced upon naturalism – and on many Bauhaus works! The neo-classical academy already displayed all the questionable elements of an artificially revivified formal repertoire: in place of form there appeared simply an empty formal scheme – thus it was that the academic teaching of the fairly recent past, enfeebled as it had been by naturalism, was no longer able to give its pupils any useful groundwork whatever. An undirected, imitative method of instruction is certainly the least satisfactory open to any art school.

It is significant that the reactions to the academic style were 'anti-naturalistic'. The Fauves, the Expressionists and the Cubists were the most recent important examples. Even the French academies ignored Impressionism and thus missed both contact with the new currents in art and the analysis of the creative means, the self-examination of the arts which goes with it, as well as all recognition of the primacy of form which solved the problem of form-and-content. In the academies it was not artistic form which had primacy, but a vague something which was called the 'object': 'head', 'nude' and 'figure in a landscape' were the celebrated academic themes. The vague significance of the 'object' corresponded with vague means, which produced vague paintings or sculptures inhabiting an unreal world between nature and artistic form. Thus the academies became the embodiment of artistic apathy and archaism. It is therefore not by chance that most of the great pace-makers in art in the late nineteenth century were self-taught, although not from choice. They included Cézanne, Van Gogh and Gauguin. Others, such as Picasso, Kandinsky and Klee, found a formal vocabulary which was both their own and contained pointers for the future precisely through their private revolt against the academies. The academies today allow their pupils a freedom which they either cannot use or which they misuse for a subjective whim; thus the academies have ceased even to be ground for revolution.

Oskar Schlemmer had the good fortune to find in Adolf Hölzel an academic teacher who stood at the centre of the artistic life of his time and whose work and teaching was forward-looking. Hölzel was not only a painter, he was also a theoretician and therefore

[3] *Adolf Hölzel. [Catalogue of the memorial exhibition for the centenary of Adolf Hölzel's birth]* (Stuttgart, 1953).

[4] Oskar Schlemmer, Diary, November 1921, page 118.

particularly well qualified to be a teacher. His own words indicate the orientation of his work and thought: 'The spirit of a work of art lies in a spiritualized use of the means.'[3] The means as such are nothing unless they serve to realize an artistic idea. An idea can be objectivized only when the artist possesses the means and eliminates everything which might hinder their application and weaken their prescriptive use. Hölzel's thesis had an enduring influence on Schlemmer; for Schlemmer's ideas were always revolving round the pictorial means and round the question of their intellectual application, of a pregnant theme: '...We possess the means but have no idea.'[4] Most academic teachers cared neither about the means nor about an intellectualized application of them.

The Bauhaus recognized the blindness and inadequacy of the academies and set out to be an anti-academic teaching institution. Gropius saw the model for such an establishment in the builders' lodges of the Middle Ages, in which master-builder, sculptor, and painter together planned and built a cathedral. The community of craftsmen and artists in the builders' lodges gave Gropius the idea of bringing craft and art together and of making the building the goal of all the arts. Timely and obvious though the idea was, it was difficult to realize.

The basic idea of the Bauhaus, the amalgamation of craft and art and co-ordination of the several arts, required a smoothly working collective. The Bauhaus teachers and pupils were not, however, equal units in a collective, but marked individualists who would not hear of fitting in and subordinating themselves in a way which would make them all equal. Each of the Bauhaus teachers tried to measure up to the Bauhaus idea in his own way, and community of idea and labour did not therefore run deep enough to prevent dissension.

The second great difficulty lay in the co-ordination of craft and art. The creative activity of the artist and the craftsman had grown apart since the last great stylistic period. Neo-classicism had only a narrow intellectual and social basis left, it was specifically academic and thus no longer embraced handicraft but only artistic handicraft. It was the academician's pride to be at the farthest remove from the craftsman and the craftsman had no access to the artist's ideas: he was merely an agent whose work was mechanical, and this often applied even to the artist craftsman. This historical rift between craft and art was aggravated in the nineteenth century by industrialization, which removed the living ground from handicraft and reduced it in the twentieth century to a relic of a vanished economic system. The ideas which artists since Impressionism had sought to objectivize were even more foreign to the craftsman than neo-classical and historicizing ideas. The craftsmen belonged to the 'people', the artist to the small, socially isolated élite which was 'in advance of its time'. Above all, now that steel and cement were used, building itself was already highly industrialized by the time the Bauhaus was started.[5] Schlemmer was for these reasons sceptical about the programme: 'Architects, sculptors, painters, we must all return to the crafts!' and its refinement: 'The artist is an exalted kind of craftsman.'[6] Thus he wrote in November 1922, when instruction in the Bauhaus workshops was already in progress: 'I do not believe in craft. We shall not reinstate medieval craft any more than medieval art, not even relatively in a corresponding modern sense. It has been overtaken by the whole of modern development. Artistic handicrafts in the age of the machine and technology become wares for the rich, lacking the broad basis of earlier times and popular roots. Industry makes today what was formerly made by hand, or will do, as its whole development indicates; we shall have standardized, solid commodities, suited to the material of which they are made.'[7] 'I do not think that craft as we practise it at the Bauhaus can transcend aestheticism to fulfil deeper social functions. Nor is "contact with industry" enough; one would have to go right in and become part of it. And that cannot be our function . . .'[8]

In fact the Bauhaus workshops did not fertilize the fine arts which were taught at the Bauhaus, but the latter did fertilize the products of the workshops. Only between the joinery workshop and the designs for interior architecture was there any close link. Work was conducted in the stone and wood carving workshops as in a sculptor's studio.

The historical link between craft and art had largely consisted in the fact that many painters and sculptors had learnt a craft (artistic) before they became painters and sculptors, but only after they had reached that stage did they add to the formal repertoire of the craft. At that time only those who possessed talent and intellect enough to break through the narrow limits of craft were able to embark upon careers as artists. It was not the craft that was the foundation of artistic creation but the special qualities which those who graduated from craft to art brought with them. The 'craft' which was taught in the sculpture and painting workshops applied exclusively to the technical concerns of these arts. The idea that craft is a 'healthy' precondition of art is merely a romantic one. A strengthening of the visual arts, such as Gropius may have had in mind during the Bauhaus period, could not proceed from craft; it could – and can – only be the result of a general intellectual change.

The idea of restoring the interconnexion between art and craft was an obvious one for architects, for they are as much bound by craft – technology – as by their artistic purposes.

It is significant that in the Bauhaus books which have already

[5] Hans M. Wingler, *The Bauhaus*, translated by Wolfgang Jabs and Basil Gilbert. Edited by Joseph Stein (The MIT Press, Cambridge, Mass., and London, 1969).

[6] Hans M. Wingler, *The Bauhaus*, page 31.

[7] Oskar Schlemmer, Diary, November 1922, page 142.

[8] Oskar Schlemmer, Diary, November 1922, page 142.

appeared there has been no mention of craft. Nor is there any reference to craft in Schlemmer's notes for his course at the Bauhaus. None could be established, for the intellectual prerequisites of craft and art are different.

It is also significant that in these books the idea of relating the arts to architecture does not receive the attention that one would have expected from the painters of the Bauhaus. Klee and Kandinsky did not concern themselves at all with the question of painting in association with architecture, Moholy-Nagy devoted only a short and extremely general chapter to the subject, while Oskar Schlemmer mentions the idea only in his diaries and letters. Many of his easel paintings are conceived as murals and his main theme, man in architecture, was also concerned with the idea of recreating an inner relationship between painting and architecture. It receives no special treatment in his notes for the preliminary course.

[9] Hans M. Wingler, *The Bauhaus*, page 31.

'The ultimate aim of all visual arts is the complete building!'[9] The opening sentence of Gropius's Bauhaus Manifesto of 1919 envisages the architectonic *Gesamtkunstwerk*. This sentence contains a greater historical truth than the one which describes the artist as an exalted kind of craftsman. The only question is how this first sentence of the programme contained in the Bauhaus Manifesto can be implemented in the twentieth century.

The architecture of the twentieth century is a specifically profane architecture — it calls itself 'objective' and 'functional' — and, its functional and formal solutions being of the best, it needs no sculpture or painting. Smooth walls 'call' for pictorial accessories only when they are not formally grounded or when provision has been made for painting or sculpture at the planning stage. The first case is the usual one, the second should have been exemplified at the Bauhaus but was not. The Dessau Bauhaus was not a combined plan by architects, painters and sculptors, it was a plan by Gropius. The walls carry neither integrally planned paintings nor sculpture, they are 'pure' architecture. This architecture is as 'pure' and 'absolute' as was the painting of Klee or Kandinsky. Oskar Schlemmer's murals for the staircase of the workshop building of the Weimar Bauhaus were carried out in the finished building executed by Van de Velde. The Bauhaus painter had to accommodate himself to existing architectonic conditions.

[10] Hans M. Wingler, *The Bauhaus*, page 31.

Architects, sculptors, painters, we all must return to the crafts! For art is not a 'profession'. There is no essential difference between the artist and the craftsman. The artist is an exalted craftsman. In rare moments of inspiration, transcending the consciousness of his will, the grace of heaven may cause his work to blossom into art. But proficiency in a craft is essential to every artist. Therein lies the prime source of creative imagination. Let us then create a new guild of craftsmen without the class distinctions that raise an arrogant barrier between craftsman and artist! Together let us desire, conceive, and create the new structure of the future, which will embrace architecture and sculpture and painting in one unity and which will one day rise toward heaven from the hands of a million workers like the crystal symbol of a new faith.[10]

Gropius wished to realize his idea by erecting a 'cathedral of socialism', but this cathedral could not be built. And since Gropius did not institute an architecture class at the Weimar Bauhaus, nor, at least until 1927, at Dessau, a total work of art could not even be conceived on paper. Schlemmer wrote: 'The building and architecture class, which was to have been the heart of the Bauhaus, does not officially exist, instead there is Gropius's private office. . . This sore and black spot is and always has been my anxiety. If the Bauhaus would profess itself a modern art school, much would become clear. It is neither one thing nor the other, perpetual unrest, open to attacks and so on.'[11] 'What I want is this: more architecture at the Bauhaus, more observance of the laws for all the rest; the Bauhaus should seek out, collect, conserve the possible laws – old and new.' 'Only this: there is no class for architecture at the Bauhaus, none of the students wants to become a master-builder, or rather none can, for this reason. Yet the Bauhaus represents the idea of the leading role of architecture . . . It is easy to compose a programme (in the abstract), very difficult to carry it out . . .'[12] This is a criticism of the roots, of the inadequate implementation of the Bauhaus programme, which places architecture at its beginning, middle and end. From the canons of architecture – in so far as they could have been established – conclusions could perhaps have been drawn about the canons of painting and sculpture and on the level of such canons a co-ordination of the arts could perhaps have taken place, or at least have been begun. Schlemmer took the programme of the Bauhaus more seriously than the other masters of his rank and so he complained: 'What worries me and disturbs my rest is the Bauhaus. Imagine the thing, with almost no fixed pole, queered from a thousand sides. It is a fact and those who come from outside confirm it, that the name of the Bauhaus arouses ideas, justifiable ones, ideas about building and buildings, and what we find is a modern school of art. Certainly it has workshops in which rough-hewing and spoon-cutting based on aesthetic sentiments goes on, somewhat better than a school of artistic handicrafts. The teaching is such as should be provided by academies which are anxious to remain viable.'[13]

Another reason why the programme of the Bauhaus was problematic was that it was planned at a time when the arts were reflecting upon themselves and upon their autonomy. The Bauhaus contributed much to this process of self-examination and in so doing fulfilled an urgent obligation of the art of the time. This demand, it is true, involved its opposite: the desire for a total work of art; but this desire was unattainable romanticism, for the intellectual preconditions for realizing it were lacking. Functional building and art were mutually exclusive.

For the arts to consider the means and elements peculiar to

[11] Oskar Schlemmer, Letter to O. M., Weimar, end of March 1922, pages 124-5.

[12] Oskar Schlemmer, Letter to O. M., Weimar, 23 June 1921, page 115.

[13] Oskar Schlemmer, Letter to O. M., end of March 1922, page 125.

themselves was the concrete path to the goal which Schlemmer saw as the duty of the Bauhaus: '. . . the Bauhaus should seek out, collect and conserve the possible laws – old and new'. In order to fulfil this duty Schlemmer looked for a point of repose at the Bauhaus; for however necessary intellectual excitement may be, reflection is necessary too. Schlemmer did not, however, mistake the significance of the unrest at the Bauhaus: 'The peculiar structure of the Bauhaus is expressed in the person of its leader: versatile, committed to no dogma, with a nose for everything new and contemporary which is stirring in the world and with the good will to assimilate it. With the good will, too, to stabilize this great whole, to bring it to a common denominator, to create a code. Hence the war of minds, public or private, such as perhaps exists nowhere else, a continual restlessness which forces individuals almost daily to take up a basic position in the face of profound problems. According to the temperament of the individual, he either suffers under this diversity or relishes it in the extreme, it either fragments him or strengthens him in his opinions.'[14] Restlessness and repose were to influence one another: restlessness a safeguard against apathy, repose to allow the intellectual factors which had been uncovered by the restlessness to mature. 'What we can do today is quiet preparatory work.'[15] This quiet work includes the search for laws. The laws which Schlemmer means must not be confused with academic rules, they are not recipes for making a work of art, but rather the work of art's objective basis, the nexus which holds together the most divergent manifestations of artistic form.

The search for the laws of form leads to the heart of the special problems of art education. Together with this search, Schlemmer wanted the Bauhaus also to assemble a 'registry of all the best from the past, formally and qualitatively, and of the present'.[16] The two tasks belong together, for laws can only be recognized retrospectively: from formal analyses of existing works and from the analysis of the artist's own works and working procedures. Since these problems touch the most difficult questions as to what is teachable in art training we will discuss them in greater detail.

At a time when art seemed to contain nothing specifically teachable, the attempt to go back to craft for the purpose of developing a new method of art teaching made sense because there were historical precedents. Regarding the fact that the fine arts once belonged among the crafts, it was, of course, forgotten that art instruction at the period of the builders' lodges, as in all the great stylistic periods, did not consist merely of transmitting a relevant technique but primarily of handing on the formal repertoire existing at the time and of following rules to ensure that it was properly applied.

[14] Oskar Schlemmer, Diary, June 1923, page 147.

[15] Oskar Schlemmer, Diary, June 1923, page 147.

[16] Oskar Schlemmer, Diary, March 1922, page 124.

By 'formal repertoire' we have to understand the formal schemes evolved in the several styles, with which the visible world – and through it the range of subjects topical at the period in question – is pictorially handled. The pupil had to learn this formal repertoire by copying drawings and finished works and by working with the master, and this taught him how to conceive a work in visual terms and to shape it; there were also norms for this purpose in every stylistic period in world art. Thus the pupil became a good or not so good painter or sculptor not only because he understood his craft – had mastered the technical prerequisites – but primarily because he had adopted the formal repertoire of the time and had learnt to apply it. Even the great geniuses of history learnt in this way.

Analysis of artistic means is in the last resort nothing more than starting to learn 'at the bottom'. It means a course of study which begins with drawing lines of different kinds in order to become familiar with the line as a means; which examines geometric figures in order to recognize their autonomy and the laws of their construction; which grapples with chiaroscuro and colour in order to become acquainted with graphic and painterly values and to draw the consequences from them.

The real importance of the Bauhaus in the field of special art instruction lies in the fact of its having included analysis of the creative means in its teaching. These means form the sole objective basis of the visual arts of the twentieth century. Even the manner in which and the purpose for which they are used are subjective, are no longer universally binding and in this fact lie the peculiar difficulties presented by this part of the Bauhaus teaching.

If students' work is to be guided in the desired intellectual direction, definite problems must be set. The Bauhaus teachers set the problems on the basis of their own experiences and the problems were therefore subjective; they were more relevant to the teachers than to the students. The teachers evolved the problems out of an imaginative over-all view, the problems were splinters of this view. The students were quite unaware of the total view, all they had to go upon was the splinter, out of which they could make little more than aesthetic shapes. This situation gave rise to a new danger: aestheticism.

The 'pure' pictorial means – line, plane, chiaroscuro and colour – and the geometrical figures which are inserted as elements of artistic form, are as such not intellectual, they have no more than decorative value. If these means and elements are not used imaginatively and intellectually and in a specifically pictorial way they lead to a certain aestheticism. This tendency is aggravated when the problem is set not from an over-all view, but is of a non-imaginative, speculative nature. For example: 'Combine a

[17] Hans M. Wingler, *The Bauhaus*, pages 438–9.

hollow cylinder, a double cone, a cube, a sphere, and a rectangular plate in a free compositional relationship.'[17] The 'free compositional relationship' is in itself a contradiction, since a 'compositional relationship' cannot be free but can only be determined by composition, and this determination is absolute. The stereometric elements are arbitrarily chosen, in the aggregate they make no sense, form no distinct figure. They cannot be composed, they can only be arranged to make a more or less pleasing configuration. It makes no difference at all whether a still life is to be 'composed' out of turnips and death's heads or whether stereometric figures are to be 'freely composed': both projects are typically academic. Kandinsky's project to abstract a 'still life' out of a table, a chair, a ladder, a table-cloth, a waste-paper basket and a bread basket[18] was equally academic: here too the arbitrary choice of objects can only result in arrangements, in aestheticism.

[18] Hans M. Wingler, *The Bauhaus*, pages 436–7.

Formal laws become discoverable only when problems such as those which have been mentioned are set in such a way that they contain the seed of a pictorial construction. The pictorial construction today must no longer follow the same lines as an academic composition, for these are historically overloaded and intellectually exhausted. Instead, the goal should be to use the chosen means and elements so that they produce a congruous pictorial figure, which derives its law of construction from the manner in which the first means (elements) are deployed. Only in this way will the field of force become visible in which form can arise.

Constructional laws of form, which can be discovered in the manner indicated, can also be extracted from existing works of pictorial art by exact formal analysis. Such analyses were made at the Bauhaus, but were not of such a fundamental and objective kind as the intended purpose demands. Itten writes of his analyses at the Bauhaus: '. . . To experience a work of art means to re-experience it, means to awaken the essential, the living quality which rests in its form, to personal life. The work of art is re-born in me.'[19] Schlemmer records: 'Itten gives "analyses" at Weimar. He shows slides from which the students are supposed to draw this or that essential element; usually the movement, the main line, the curve. Then he refers to a Gothic figure. After that he shows the weeping Mary Magdalene from Grünewald's altarpiece; the students strive to separate some essential feature from the very complex configuration. Itten sees their attempts and thunders: "If you had any artistic sensibility you would not draw in the presence of this sublime image of weeping, which could be the weeping of the world, you would sit there and burst into tears." So saying he slams the door!'[20] No formal laws can be discovered in this inexact and emotionally overcharged manner.

[19] Johannes Itten, 'Analyses of old masters', in H. M. Wingler, *The Bauhaus*, page 49.

[20] Oskar Schlemmer, Letter to O. M., 16 May 1921, page 112.

19

Analysis of pictorial form is more than an approximate copying of 'essential' elements. It was essential, however, that such analyses were thought of at all.

As the quotations show, Schlemmer saw the situation at the Bauhaus clearly and he was much concerned with the problems, both soluble and insoluble. His ethical nature moved him to bring clarity to the confusion of the Bauhaus and to take his own bearings. 'A change from abstract to non-abstract pictorial means has almost become a symptom of the age, even here at the Bauhaus. I myself have been overtaken by it and am trying to bring order to the whole situation, so that the two can exist side by side and live together, one no less than the other, if there is reason for it, and that people should know why a thing is done in this way or that.'[21]

[21] Oskar Schlemmer, Diary, 25 June 1923, page 148.

An attempt to achieve a synthesis of apparently divergent tendencies also characterizes the notes Schlemmer left for his preliminary course on *man* presented here. Concentration on a single theme — representation of the human being — enabled him to set wide limits to his teaching and to include everything which he thought important, so as to be able to elaborate it without losing the thread. His teaching was to be the rallying-point of all the elements at the Bauhaus which he thought significant and of all that was still lacking to give the students the feeling that they were receiving a complete course of instruction. In March 1928 Schlemmer wrote to his wife: 'In future I shall have the theme "man" as the subject of my teaching. I must find all sorts of literature on the subject. It is a gigantic field and I must adjust to it, to do, from within, everything that interests me. For I shall have to occupy and hold the attention of the third semester: Kandinsky the first, Klee the second, myself the third. Theory of descent, theory of race, sexual biology, ethics and so on. Or so at least I imagine. Something that has been lacking at the Bauhaus until now.'[22] Over and above the teaching of the material, his endeavour had a clearly defined goal which transcended the subjects he was to teach: 'It is true that I am curious to know where it will lead, how the theory of life will look by the end of the semester, whether it will be possible to build something out of the opinions of the warring scholars and philosophers which is personal and universal. It will not, I think, be love's labour lost and will in some sense be a contribution or more to universal, personal views.'[23] Schlemmer's wish to impart a philosophical outlook on life to the students of the Bauhaus originated in the lack of a theory of life; and this lack was the cause of many shortcomings in art education, the main cause of the intellectual and artistic shortcomings under which even the Bauhaus had to labour.

[22] Oskar Schlemmer, Letter to T., Dessau, 1 March 1928, page 232.

[23] Oskar Schlemmer, Diary, end of May 1928, pages 235–6.

The Bauhaus, certainly, did not serve directly as a model for an art school, but it showed that it was possible to discover in principle new lines for art education. The time allotted to the Bauhaus was too short for final judgement to be passed on the significance, on the artistic and pedagogic potentialities of these lines. What Oskar Schlemmer wrote about the path of the individual artist is true also of the paths of art teaching : 'There is no universal recipe for all paths. In the first place there is only the path of the individual answerable to himself. He may remain a lone traveller, or his path may become a highway. The original is usually identical with the elementary and the latter with the simple. We can always begin over again with the ABC, we can always reconsider the elements of art, because in simplicity there is a strength in which every true innovation is rooted. Simplicity, understood as what is elementary and typical, out of which diversity and individuality evolve organically, simplicity understood as tabula rasa and a general purging of all the eclectic accessories of every style and period, must surely guarantee that path which we call the future !'[24]

[24] Oskar Schlemmer, Diary, April 1926.

Oskar Schlemmer's conception of man

[1] Thus Schlemmer describes man in his syllabus 'Subject of instruction: man'.

Oskar Schlemmer saw man not as an 'objective' motif, he saw him as a psychophysical whole, to which his chief obligation as an artist lay. He regarded man as a 'cosmic being',[1] a world-totality, and this view of man was doubtless the most powerful spur to his impassioned and tireless efforts to evolve a valid artistic form for man as he saw him in and from his time. The things of the visible world acquire an intellectual meaning for the artist only when they are freed from their isolated 'objectivity' and are viewed 'cosmically' — to maintain Schlemmer's terminology — together with man and the whole world. The 'object' is nothing if it is to be merely an isolated thing; only in a universal system of references does it gain significance, become a quantity which obliges man to come to terms with it. Indeed, man himself gains in the eye of the artist that considerable significance which he had in the great periods of western art only when he sees him not simply as a mere 'object' but as a 'cosmic being'. As such he is both a totality in himself and a part of a larger totality, of the cosmos, which may be regarded as a universal system of references. The concept 'cosmos' embraces the idea of a universal order, an order of an intellectual kind — and this is the artist's concern.

Schlemmer's assessment of man as a 'cosmic being', his attempt to project a rounded image of man, indicate that he conceived his teaching on man from a metaphysical point of view. It seems to be in the nature of the artist to incline towards metaphysics, often, indeed, towards mysticism. Only when he views the world from an angle which raises it above mere matter does the artist see it as worthy of creative effort. Oskar Schlemmer also spoke of a 'mystical bent' in himself.[2] He was, however, fully aware of the danger of this bent towards mysticism and he reflected: 'To strive for: truth, no humbug, no meaningless mysticism, the forms of reality in the service of art.'[3] The outcome of that bent towards

[2] Oskar Schlemmer, Diary, 16 April 1928.
[3] Oskar Schlemmer, Diary, 28 November 1919, page 84.

mysticism which Germans so often possess to a dangerously pronounced degree was to show itself in Schlemmer's case in a metaphysical view of life, in which it was able to work itself out productively. The criterion of this view of life lies not in propositions which can be verified by scholastic logic, but in its consequences for artistic creativity, in the question whether it helps or hinders. A painter or sculptor is not in a position to build up a view of the world by speculative means, and since there was in Schlemmer's day no binding view of the world, he sought counsel from kindred spirits, from poets, and accepted from them what had affinities with his own sensibility and feeling. As the heir of the great German artists, Schlemmer saw man involved in the cosmos and the cosmos bearing upon man, for: 'The cosmos is a trinity made up of mind, nature and soul; these three essences exist only in mutual association. Nature is corporeal and materializes in the domain of space, the mind is the inner aspect of nature and is timeless and spaceless, the soul is the connecting agent and moves in the domain of time' wrote Ricarda Huch in her book *Vom Wesen des Menschen (On the nature of man)*,[4] to which Schlemmer's metaphysical view is related.

[4] Ricarda Huch, *Vom Wesen des Menschen, Natur und Geist.* (Munich 1922), page 1.

To make this view, this image of man, intelligible to his pupils, Schlemmer developed the classes on nude and figure drawing which accompanied his 'Course on man'. Instruction in the sciences was to help to achieve this aim. The sciences were to demonstrate in their own way that man is a 'cosmic being'. The natural sciences were to show that man is an integral part of nature. The theories of philosophy are an attempt by man to know himself and the world and to understand that all that exists is one. Psychology was to give an insight into the structure of man's psyche and his attitude to the world.

Among the geometrical figures with which the human form may be represented Schlemmer includes 'line, which connects sight with what is seen, ornament, which takes shape between a body and the exterior world, symbolizing the relationship of the one to the other'.[5]

[5] Oskar Schlemmer, Diary, October 1915, page 43.

Syllabuses – Teaching schedules

Oskar Schlemmer
Subject of instruction: man
Compulsory for third semester, 2 weekly periods, 21 double periods in all.

The representation of the human body has hitherto been restricted to *drawing of the nude*. This was extended in the winter of 1927/28 to include *figure drawing* (schematic representation of the human body as line, plane, body, according to number, measurement and proportion: as skeleton, according to musculature, etc.) and was completed from the summer of 1928 onwards by the class on *man*.

It is essential for the 'new life', which should express itself as a modern feeling about the world and life, that man should be understood as a *cosmic being*. His conditions of existence, his relationships with the natural and artificial environment, his mechanism and organism, his material, spiritual and intellectual image; in short, man as a bodily and spiritual being is a necessary and important subject of instruction.

The subject is divided into three parts, the *formal*, the *biological* and the *philosophical* part, which correspond to graphic representation, scientific structure and the transcendental world of ideas. In the classes the three parts run concurrently and are studied in turn so that they combine at the end to suggest the totality of the concept *man*.

The part on figural representation, which is mainly concerned with drawing, deals with the norms and systems of line, plane and solidity or plasticity: standard measurements, theories of proportion, Dürer's measurement and the Golden Section. These lead on to the laws of movement, the mechanics and kinetics of the body, both within itself and in space, both in natural space and in civilized space (building). Much weight is naturally given to the latter theme: the relationship of man to his habitation and its furnishing, to domestic appliances. The ways of movement, the choreography of everyday, lead on to deliberate, organized movement in gymnastics and dance and beyond to the art of the theatre (q.v.). This section closes with analyses of figural representations in early and modern art.

The scientific part begins with the enigmas of the world, ether and plasma, and discusses cytology and embryology, birth and growth, life and death, the articulation of the skeleton, the function of the muscles, the internal organs, the heart as a pump for circulating the blood, the lungs and respiration, the intestines and metabolism, the sexual and sense organs, brain and nerves. All these are explained from the biochemical and biomechanical viewpoint, and in this connexion questions of food, hygiene and clothing are touched upon. The senses of touch and sight are naturally of special importance: the factual world of anatomy, the theory of the structure of the body, are here contrasted with the less unambiguous physiology and the theory of the vital activities, leading on to the third, the philosophical, approach.

The function of the philosophical part is to present man the thinking and feeling being, the world of imagination, concepts, ideas, the struggles for a philosophy of life. A short survey of the basic systems of thought from antiquity until modern times, with special mention of the concept of substance, conceptions of time and space and not least the nature of the *psyche*, ends with the metaphysical knowledge to elucidate questions of aesthetics and ethics. Despite all attempts at objectivity in reference to these expositions it will be impossible to prevent the teacher's subjective approach, current trends and the claims of the day exerting their influence on the resultant view of the world. The point and purpose of the exercises will be to persuade students to form their own view of the world, which must be the world of today.

In all three parallel subjects importance will be attached to the making of illustrative, easily remembered, drawn and painted schemata and diagrams, so that, for example, even processes of thought, scales of feeling, will be presented in line and colour. Thus theories of form and colour learnt in previous courses will find an application in relating and structuring ideas.

Subject of instruction: nude drawing
Compulsory for third semester. Optional for all. 2 periods weekly, 21 double periods in all.

The class on 'man' is preceded on the evening of the previous day by drawing from the living model. In default of good models the students help themselves and take it in turn to act as model. This ensures a great variety of bodies. Then the nude drawing is transferred to the stage or *aula*, which means that instead of the dull class-room and unvarying monotonous lighting, stimulation and variety are created by structures, apparatus, spotlights and sometimes even gramophone music. The nude posture for the evening, as long as it is a stationary posture held for one or two hours and not a quick sequence of movements, is analysed on the blackboard during the break and the essential features, basic forms, axes of movement, bone structure and musculature, light and shade are stressed.

Subject of instruction: stage theory
Compulsory for students in the theatre department. 2 periods weekly, 21 double periods in all.

Exploration of the elementary theatrical means will throw new light upon the possibility of invention and structure. These elements are (in conformity with the idea of the Bauhaus) first and foremost: form and colour, space, movement, speech and sound, idea and composition. Every other event on the stage, be it independent or human, arises out of them: form as linear, plane, three-dimensional (wings, properties, costumes); colour as coloured form, as coloured light, transparency, projection and shadow; space in its dimensions, the possibility of varying it by division and movement; movement itself, the mechanical movement of forms and the organic movement of man in dance and pantomime; speech as abstract sound, communicating word, structured song; the musical sound of the instruments and devices; the idea which uses the available means to form and compose optical, mechanical, acoustic and dramatic events.

Theoretical knowledge of theatrical means runs parallel with practical work on the stage (more detailed exposition in No. 3/1927 of the *Bauhaus Journal*, special number 'Bühne').

The results of the practical work are recorded in line and colour in the form of choreography, diagram and score.

Cosmos   Mind   the inner aspect of nature   time = spaceless
          Nature   physically manifest
          Psyche   in the domain of space

Woman
consciously temporal

Man
self-consciously intellectual

Nourishment, propagation
(Child, nature)
unconsciously childlike [?] people

Power of imagination
Will-power   Greek ideal
Energy

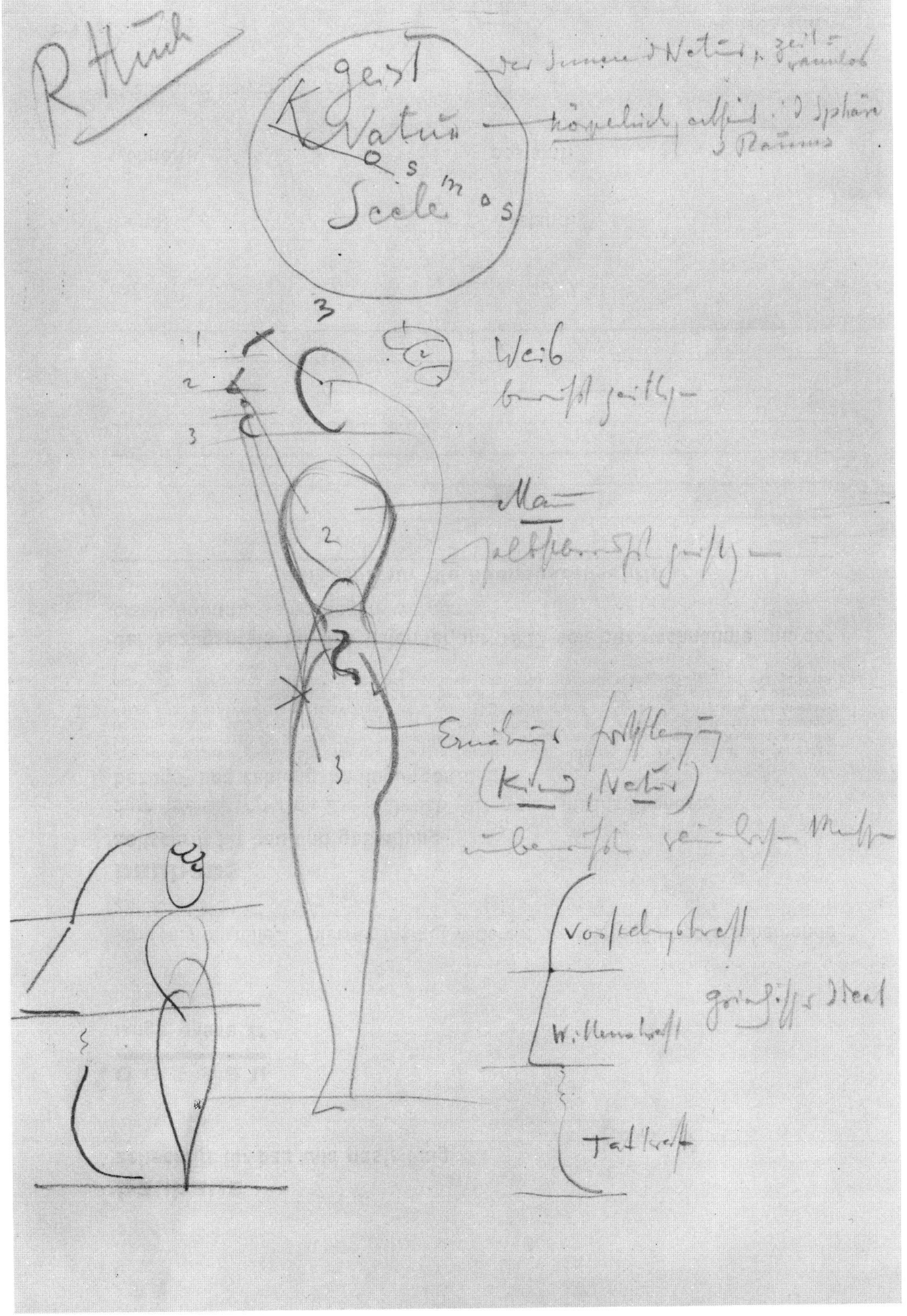
Geist
Natur
Seele
Weib
Mann
Vorstellungskraft
Willenskraft
Tatkraft

We the modern moderns!

Subject of instruction *man*. Compulsory for third semester. 2 periods weekly.

The aim is to familiarize students with man the total being and to approach this from two sides.

The visible manifestation and its representation, thus linear outline and plastic drawing of the body, in a form reduced to the simplest line, then measurement and proportion (Dürer's, Leonardo's theory of proportion, Golden Section), then presentation of mechanics and kinetics [?], its laws of movement, possibilities and limits in itself in free (natural) space and in confined (artificial) space. Diagrams of movement, choreography.

Theoretical instruction is supplemented by practical in the form of nude drawing (2 hrs. weekly). In default of good nude models and in order to gain the greatest possible variation in the figure, the students themselves act as models. The scene is the house stage, so as to get away from the dreariness of the classroom, so lighting can be varied (spotlights, shadow etc.). During the break the nude posture of the moment is analysed on the blackboard. Parallel with the mechanistic approach to the human body runs the biological approach; it begins with the history of the embryo and its development, embracing the whole chemical, psychiatric system.

Man's proportion to the proportions of the environment is an insight into furnishing, housing.

Work schedule:

	origin of man	
	history of his development	
	theory of race	
	sexual biology	
	theory of hygiene	
	relationship with air, light, warmth, clothing	
	habitation − diseases and defence	
	nervous system	
	physical and intellectual activity / psychical life	
compulsory third semester	transformations of man in the history of art	2 periods

Instruction on man

	Drawing of the nude	**Figure drawing**	
	exterior appearance	theory of proportion	
optional	plasticity / modelling	anatomy	2 alternating
	light and shadow	biomechanics	periods

	Stage Theory	
optional	Man in the space of the stage	
	dramatization	2 periods
	his environment/ the scene	

Stage

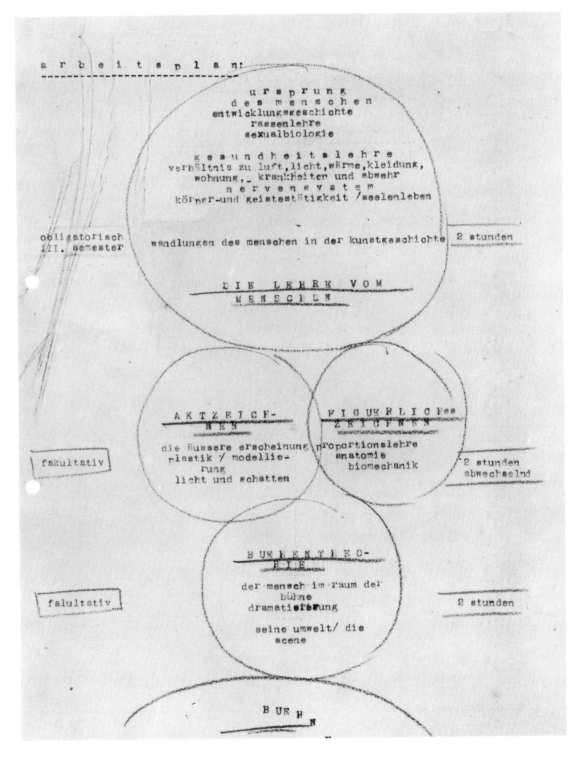

u r s p r u n g
d e s   m e n s c h e n
entwicklungsgeschichte
rassenlehre
sexualbiologie

g e s u n d h e i t s l e h r e
verhältnis zu luft,licht,wärme,kleidung,
wohnung,_ krankheiten und abwehr
n e r v e n s y s t e m
körper-und geistestätigkeit /seelenleben

wandlungen des menschen in der kunstgeschichte   2 stunden

obligatorisch
III. semester

D I E   L E H R E   V O M
M E N S C H E N

A K T Z E I C H -
N E N

die äussere erscheinung
plastik / modellie-
rung
licht und schatten

fakultativ

F I G U E R L I C H es
Z E I C H N E N

proportionslehre
anatomie
biomechanik

2 stunden
abwechselnd

B U E H E N T H E O -
R I E

der mensch im raum der
bühne
dramatisierung

seine umwelt/ die
scene

falultativ

2 stunden

B U E H N

31

die lehre vom menschen
----
arbeitsgebiete

I. entstehungsgeschichte - entwicklungsgeschichte / kurvatur des lebens / jahres-monats-tages-
kurven / rythmus der sieben/ - "woher kommen wir? wer sind wir? wohin
gehen wir?-

* II. lineare darstellung / gerade linien/ gebogene linien/
statik des körpers/ mechanik und kinetik des
körpers/

* III. mass / proportion / typen (goldener schnitt, dürer u.a.)

* IV. knochengerüst

* V. muskel - und gefässsüsteme

* VI. zellen, gewebe, fie inneren organe.

X VII. nervensystem, sinnesorgane, blutkreislauf.

* VIII. mensch und raum, orientierung, geh-und bewegungskurven,
choreographie.

— IX. leibesübungen , gymnastik, tanz, sport. rythmus.

— X. ernährung, kleidung, hygiene.

* XI. der mensch in der kunst , formale wandlungen, typen)

XII. die weltanschauung , philosophie/ die seele ,
psychologie, mechanik des geisteslebens, bewusstsein.

XIII. hypnose, suggestion, metaphysik, mystik.

= akt-und figurenzeichnen

29.3.28

Instruction on man

Subjects of work

I. **History of his origin** – history of his development/ **curvature of life**/ curves of the year, month, day/ rhythm of seven/ – 'Where do we come from ? Who are we ? Where are we going ?' –

II. **Linear representation**/ straight lines/ curved lines/ statics of the body/ mechanics and kinetics of the body.

III. **Measurement**/ **proportion**/ **types** (Golden Section, Dürer and others).

IV. **Skeleton.**

V. **Musculature and vascular systems.**

VI. **Cells, cell-tissue, the internal organs.**

VII. **Nervous system,** sense organs, circulation of the blood.

VIII. **Man and space,** orientation, curves of walking and movement, choreography.

IX. **Physical exercises,** gymnastics, dance, sport. Rhythm.

X. **Food, clothing, hygiene.**

XI. **Man in art,** formal changes, types.

XII. **Philosophy of life,** philosophy/ the psyche, psychology, mechanism of the spiritual life, consciousness.

XIII. Hypnosis, suggestion, metaphysics, mysticism.

=drawing of the nude and figure drawing

29.3.28

Normative	Biological	Philosophical
simple forms type	history of origins (ether and mass)	designation of concepts
measurements and proportion	history of development (plasma, cells, embryo)	monism – dualism
mechanics of the body, joints, skeleton and musculature		concept of substance
kinetics, gymnastics, clothing	respiration, skin, circulation of the blood	materialism – realism idealism
man and space	internal organs, metabolism, food	space and time
man and environment	brain and nerves	the psyche (feeling, will, imagination)
man and art	sense organs (sense of taste and sight)	aesthetics – ethics

Schedule Summer Semester 1928

normativ formel	biologisch...	...philosophisch
1 die einfachen formen, der typus	2 entstehungsgeschichte (äther und masse)	3 begriffbestimmungen
4 maasse und proportion	5 entwicklungsgeschichte (plasma, zelle, keim)	6 monismus- dualismus
7 körpermechanik, gelenke, skelett und muskulatur	8	9 . der substanzbegriff
kinetik, gymnastik kleidung	atmung, haut, blutkreislauf	materialismus-realismus idealismus
mensch und raum	innere organe, stoffwechsel ernährung	raum und zeit
mensch und umwelt	hirn und nerven	die seele (gefühl, wille, vorstelln
mensch und kunst	sinnesorgane (tast-u. sehsinn	ästhetik- ethik

Plan Sommer Semester 1928

Week	Man	Stage theory	Man (descr.)
1	General : over-all schedule, drawing of same, history of development, General, cosmic man	General : over-all schedule, drawing of same	General Cosmic man
2	The simple forms, norms, formal figuration (line, plane, body), simplest measurements	The simple forms, norms, formal figuration line, surface, body	The simple forms
3	Theory of proportion (Schmidt, Dürer, Golden Section), theory of types	Stage measurements, normalization	World evolution, plasma
4	Mechanics of the body (a) static movement	ditto of forms	Theories of proportion
5	Mechanics of the body (b) kinetic movement (M. and time)	ditto of forms	Plasma, cells
6	Organic : bone structure and system, anatomy		Skeleton
7	Organic, anatomy, the internal organs, the intestines		Designation of concept philosophy etc.
8	Organic, anatomy (muscular, vascular, skin system, circulation of the blood)		Skeleton, musculature
9	Nervous system, sense organs		
10	Man and space (a) natural space (b) artificial space curves of movement		
11	Physical exercises : gymnastics, sport, dance (rhythm creative pause)		
12	Clothing, food, hygiene		
13	Man and art formal changes intellectual changes		
14	The human psyche Psychology Mechanics of the intellectual life		
15	View of the world and of life Philosophy		
16	Hypnosis, suggestion, metaphysics, mysticism		
17	Practice		

	Woche	Mensch	Bühnentheorie	Mensch. (erl.)
13.4	1	Allgemeines: Gesamtplan, Zeichng desselben, Einteilung desselben. Allgemeines kosmischer Mensch	Allgemeines: Gesamtplan, Zeichng. desselben	o Allgemeines. + Kosmischer Mensch.
20.4	2	Die einfachen Formen, Normen, formale Gestaltung (Linie, Fläche, Körper) einfache Maasse	Die einfachen Formen, Normen, formale Gestaltung (Linie, Fläche, Körper)	+ Die einfachen Formen.
27.4	3	Proportionslehre (Mensch, Tiere, Goldn. Schnitt) Typenlehre	Bühnenmasse, Menschbewegung	o Weltentwicklung. Plasma.
4.5	4	Mechanik d. Körpers a) Statische Bewegung	No d. Formen	+ Proportionslehre.
11.5	5	Mechanik d. K. b) Kinetische Bewegung (Mit. Zeit)	sto d. Formen	o Plasma, Zelle.
18.5	6	Organik; Knochenbau = System Anatomie		+ Skelett
25.5	7	Organik, Anatomie Die inneren Organe d. Eingeweide		× Begriffbestimmungen Philosophie sa.
1.6	8	Organik Anatomie c) Blutkreislauf, Hautsystem, Blutkreislauf		+ Skelett, Muskelsystem
8.6	9	Nervensystem, Sinnesorgane		o
15.6	10	Mensch = Raum a) Naturraum b) Kunstraum Bewegungsstudien		+
22.6	11	Leibesübungen: Gymnastik Sport Rhythmik, Gesch. Spiel, Tanz		o
29.6	12	Kleidung, Ernährung, Hygiene ect.		+
6.7	13	Mensch = Kunst formale Beziehungen ideelle "		o
13.7 ferien	14	Die Seele d. Mensch Psychologie Mensch u. d. Geistesleben		+
7.9	15	Die Welt, Lehre v. aussermensch. Philosophie		o
14.9	16	Hypnose, Suggestion Metaphysik u. Mystik		+
21.9	17	Übungen		o
28.9	18	"		+
5.10	19	"		o
12.10	20			+
19.10	21			o

History of human origins

History of development – curvature of life (in 7 phases)
Curve of the year – curve of the month – curve of the day
Where do we come from?
Who are we?
Where are we going?
  2 Norms, the formal
  3 Types, proportion
  4 Statics
  5 Kinetics, mechanics
  6 Cells and cell tissue
    History of the development of the whole body
  7 Skeleton
  8 Muscular and vascular system
  9 The intestines, bowel, respiration, sex
10 Nervous system and sense organs
11 Man and space (orientation)
    Curves of walking and movement
    Choreography
    Distance
    Image and recognition at distance of 1, 2, 3, 10, 20, 100 m (photos)
12 Physical exercises
    Gymnastics, dance, sport
    Rhythm, creative pause
13 Man in art
    (Formal changes – ideal type)
14 The human psyche
    Psychology – mechanics of the spiritual life – consciousness
15 Attitude to life, the world – philosophy
16 Hypnotism and suggestion – metaphysics – mysticism
17 Clothing – food – hygiene

Clear pictorial development, as it were, comprehension of man. The linear-static framework is given life, resulting necessities.

Fundamentally everything based on self-observation, demonstration, fact.

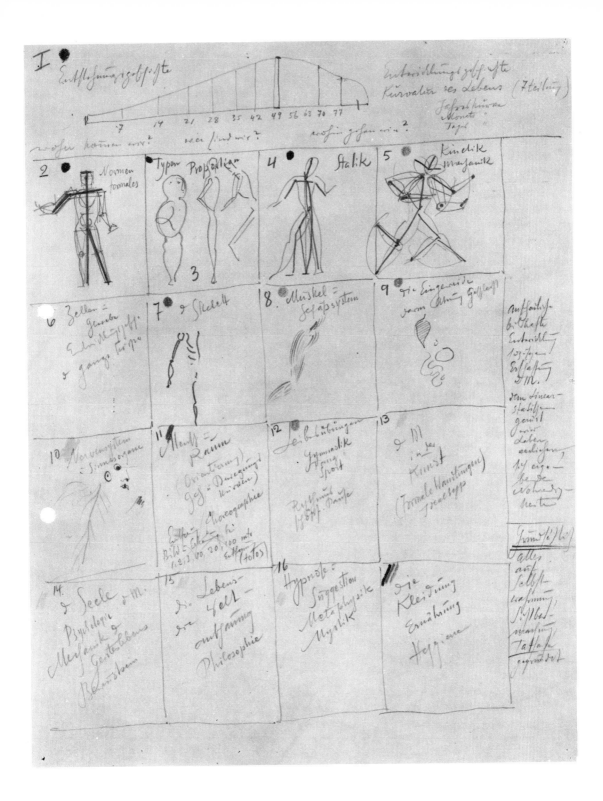

Drawing from the nude

On 16 May 1921 Oskar Schlemmer wrote in a letter to his wife: 'Gropius says he would like to start drawing from the nude for sculptors and would I take it over. I have agreed gladly and he says he will propose it. They should study the nude. Something may come of this, I am pleased about it.'[1]

[1] Oskar Schlemmer, Letter to T., 16 May 1921, page 112.

Drawing from the nude was the first preliminary course at the Bauhaus to be assigned to Schlemmer. It was, indeed, the one which was weighed down by academicism and therefore lacked the topicality of the other preliminary courses. In February 1925 Schlemmer noted in his diary: 'Drawing from the nude has fallen into disrepute among the moderns. The odium of academicism clings hard to it, no wonder, when the art now in vogue aims at the dissolution of form, deformation, anti-naturalism. So what do we look for from the nude today? Learning to draw at least – drawing from the nude takes this for granted – this can be learnt initially from inanimate nature and the living things of everyday life. It does not need to be the nude model for the student to feel after a form and reproduce it. Nor the manner of the reproduction – the ability to draw, in this or that style. The student must master all this before he confronts the nude. Understand the nude as, so to speak, the highest nature, the finest articulation and organization, as an edifice of flesh, muscles, bones. The greatest variety of attitudes are possible, I would wish for the most objective. Matisse: to be able to draw like Dürer before expressions are composed. Therefore set expressions aside, and so work towards objectivity. (Example Matisse.) "Expression too is objective." True, if by that is understood marked rhythm, elaboration of certain parts which are essential and specially striking – the inner, imaginary structure, not the scientifically correct dissecting of bones – the muscular system, too, not anatomically exact, but rather the bearer of the functions of the fleshly edifice. The more objective the study, the greater will be the student's success in elaborating this. Knowledge of the actual muscles alone enables the artist to intellectualize them and make them serve purposes beyond mere correctness. 'In front of the model, therefore, draw as correctly as possible and create the expression from memory.

'No cheap effects, trying out of mannerisms – in India ink, let alone in colour. Draw to as large a size as possible, not too small. Relate the drawing to the size of the surface. This is already composition, as far as it goes.

'Those who have the attitude, should seek to satisfy its demands as precisely as possible, those who have not should try to find the one that suits them.'[2]

[2] Oskar Schlemmer, Diary, February 1925 (unpublished).

These ideas are best illustrated by the drawings from the nude which Schlemmer himself made at the Bauhaus. They stand out from the academic drawings from the nude common at the time in that they do not spring from a vain endeavour to provide an optically 'faithful' rendering of the model. Schlemmer's 'objective attitude' consists in the fact that he fixes the static or dynamic structure and the plastic contour of the body with a largely unblurred line used as 'pure means'. Use of the pure line compels the artist to a process of abstraction. The progression of the lines cannot correspond with the contours of the body, it cannot be optical, for line, if its special character be heeded, has an autonomous relationship with surface, which Schlemmer demonstrates in a rhythmic lineation. His rhythmic management of line is, however, not expression, for it conforms strictly to the model and is not emotionally exaggerated. Rhythm is the means by which all kinds of movement are delineated. As 'pure' line is an abstraction of the contours of the body, so is a rhythmic progression of lines, receiving its impulse from the model, an abstraction of movements – of both the active movement of the model and the moving progression of the contours of the body and of the interior formations of the body.

This style of drawing, which is not a rigid mannerism, permitted Schlemmer's attitude towards the model to be objective: it allowed him to pay exact attention to the facts of its construction – and yet to satisfy the demands of artistic necessity, to translate reality into pure pictorial means, of which rhythm is one, and in this way to create a new, intellectual image of reality. His further requirement that the drawing from the nude should be related to the size of the surface on which it is drawn is also an artistic necessity: all pictorial representation is an intellectual and visual organization. As the physiological movement of the body is rhythmically organized, so is the drawing of the nude compositionally organized as a whole on the picture plane.

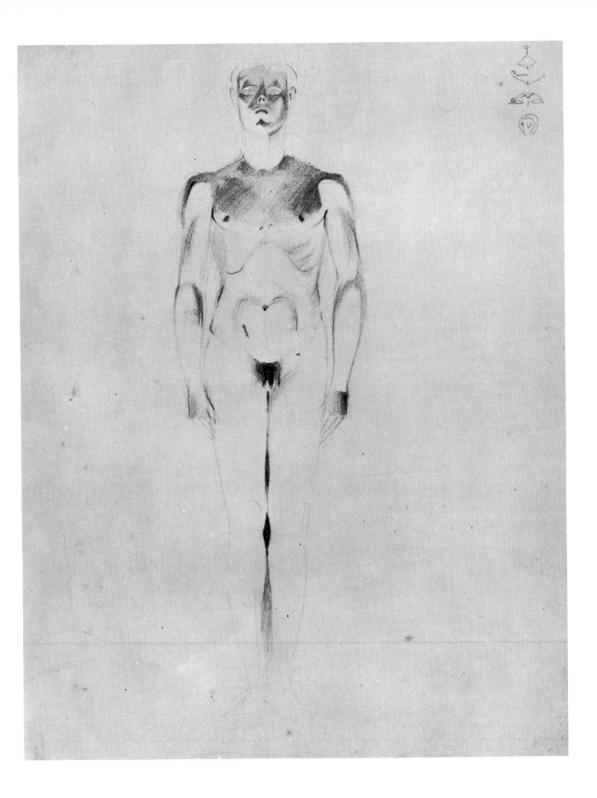

43

49

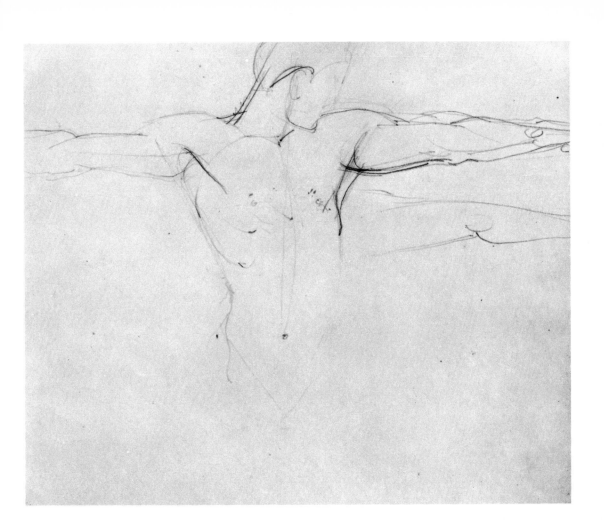

Modell: Menzel 22.11.28

52

Measurement and proportion

All the great European and non-European stylistic periods have had their own systems of measurement and proportion which applied to all the arts and contributed much to the unity of the total work of art. The last significant attempt in this direction is Le Corbusier's modulor. Mathematically established measurement did not, however, precede authentic artistic creation, it was rather derived from it. Artistic measurement – the smallest unit of size, on which the formal extension and proportioning of a figure or a figural complex (architecture) depends – is primarily imaginative. It is the expression of a particular feeling about life, of an idea, and it therefore varies from style to style. When canonized, it becomes a system which contributes to the formal unity of a style.

Schlemmer, searching for an objective basis for his subjective formal vocabulary, was concerned, particularly as a teacher, with the traditional systems of measurement of the human figure, but he recognized the limits of the usefulness of such systems: 'Certainly, there is geometry, the Golden Section, the theory of proportion. They are dead and unproductive when they are not experienced, sensed. We must allow ourselves to be surprised by the wonder of proportions, the splendour of numerical relationships and harmonies and in this way create laws out of our findings.'[1]

This section contains an exact representation of the Golden Section and the equations deriving from it, of the Egyptian system of measurement, of the Canon according to Polycles and Leonardo and especially Dürer's measurements; also representations of the shifts in proportion from the embryo to the fully grown man and anthropological systems of measurement (C. Schmidt, G. Buschan, C. G. Carus). The sheets signed O.S. are Schlemmer's own studies of proportion.

[1] Oskar Schlemmer, Diary, July–August 1923, page 150.

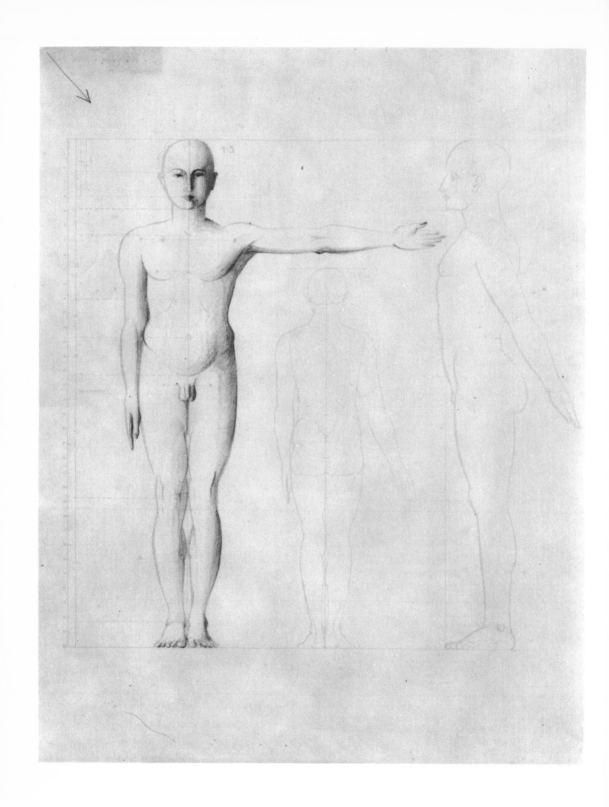

O.S.: Viereck-Teilung (horizontal·vertikal) oder Schachtelmensch

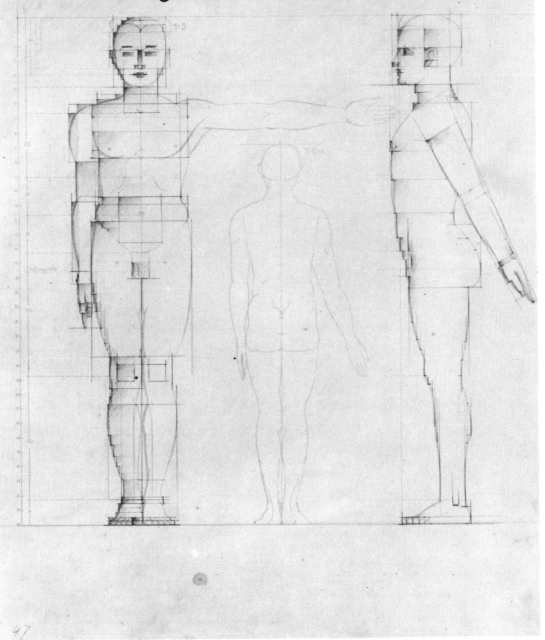

O.S. : Rectangular division (horizontal-vertical) or box man.

10

Aus Dürer's „Buch der Messung"

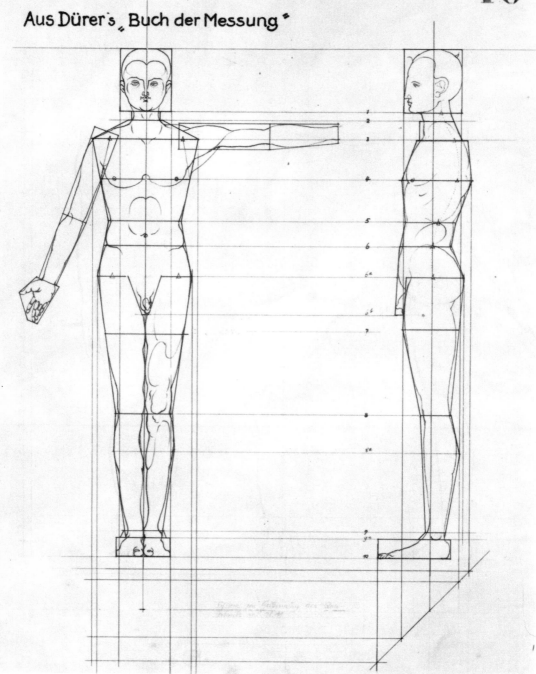

From Dürer's *Book of Measurement.*

59

Human canon

By heads – by the unit of the spinal column

The length of the **spinal column** amounts to $4/_{10}$ of the length of the body. Projected on to the profile of the body it gives tip of the nose – upper edge of breast-bone – lower edge of breast-bone – end of breast-bone – navel – pubis. Each section exactly $1/_{10}$.

Normal man 7½ **head lengths**, also 7¼–7¾
With Michelangelo – Leonardo 8
Apollo Belvedere 8½
Botticelli and the Gothic 9–10

Tallest man to date height 278 cm (Winkelmaier, an Austrian), the smallest man 38 cm (60-year-old Hilany Apybe of Sinai).

The **Egyptians** discovered that the body is **19 times longer than the middle finger** and sized their figures accordingly. Polycles first established the Canon (of the human body) – then Dürer ('Von der Gliedmass des Menschen') – Leonardo ('Trattato della pittura') – Schadow ('Polyklet') – Carus ('Symbolik der menschlichen Gestalt') – Zeising ('Proportionen nach dem Goldenen Schnitt') – Fritsch the anatomist and T. Schmidt the painter ('Proportionsschlüssel') with the spinal column as the unit of measurement, C. Schmidt 1849, Proportionsschlüssel, page 9.

Greek measurements by **hands**
(2 hands = 1 head)
2 hands = height of face
            height of breast
            breast – navel
            navel – end of trunk
3 hands = height of skull
            length of foot
4 hands = shoulder – ulna
            ulna – finger-tip
            ear-hole – navel
6 hands = navel – knee
            length of trunk
            length of thigh

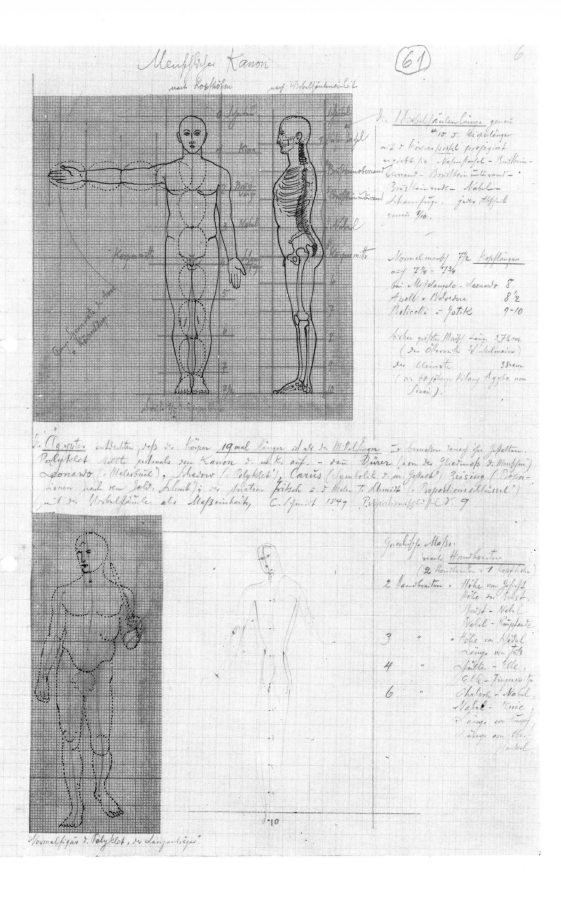

A few important points resulting from the **'Golden Section'**
(mainly concerning the length)

7th cervical vertebra – larynx – lower chin

Cleft of the shoulders

Waist

Fork of the legs,
bottom end of the ischium (side)

Finger-tip with arm hanging

Knee bent

Construction of the 'Golden Section' gives the equation:
$bc : ac = ac : ab$
(Bisect ab, perpendicular at b, arc ed with b as centre, describe a d, arc with
d as centre (db), point of intersection f, a f arc with a as centre gives c.)

Einige wesentliche Punkte, die der *Goldene Schnitt* ergibt.

(Beziehen sich i.d. Hauptsache auf die *Längenmaße*)

B

B

D

D — 7. Halswirbel Kehlkopf mit Kinn

Achselhöhle

C

C — Taille

F

F — Spaltung d. Beine, unteres Ende des Sitzknochen (Seite)

G

g — Fingerspitze b. hangendem Arm

E

E — Knie etwa knapp

a   g   c   b

Konstruktion des „Goldenen Schnitts"

ergibt Gleichung:
$$bc : ac = ac : ab$$

Nehmen ab, lot in b, Kreisbogen cd um b,
ziehe ad, Kreis um d (db), schneidet
f, ef, auf Kreisbogen um a ergibt c.

a   Mitte   b

major   minor

Simplest construction of the head from the front (O. S.)

Circle and straight line

Golden Section $ac : cb$
                        $cb = d^1 d^2$
                        $cb = a$ (tip of nose)

g = centre of the main circle of the profile (previous page)

Given ab = length of face 24 cm (circle with c as centre and $r = ac$), Golden
Section gives root of nose c circle and square $d^1 - d^6$, circle with c as centre
and $r = ac$ gives e = lower edge of lip.
Diagonals $d^1 d^3$ and $d^2 d^4$ and axes $d^5 d^6$ give lower edge of nose d.
Points of intersection of the diagonals and circle with d as centre give, above,
the outer corners of the eyes and the beginning of the neck h^1, h^2.
The ear o^1, o^2 is found in the side area formed by the circle ae and the square
$d^1 - d^4$.

Simplest construction of the head (profile) (O.S.)

Circle and straight line
and plastic representation
Sphere
Cube
Cylinder
Root of nose
Centre of eye
Height of ear

See how many parts of the square *a*, *d*, *e*, *c* have to be lengthened downwards
to get the proportion of the face.

Given : length of head 24 cm $= bf$
4 parts of the same give $r = ab$
Horizontal *ad* gives root of nose,
Diagonal *ah* and arc *dh* give cranium
Square *a*, *d*, *e*, *c* $+ \,^1/_9$ length of head gives *a*, *d*, *g*, *f* as 'area of face'

$a =$ beginning of ear
Point $b =$ end of ear
$ce =$ height of chin

Einfachste
Kopfkonstruktion (Kopf) O.Si.

Kreis u. Gerade

Zur plastischen
Darstellung

Kugel
Kubus
Cylinder

21 cm

b

1

2

3

d   a

5

6

7   h   24 cm

8

e   c

g   f 9

Zu untersuchen, wieviel Teile des Quadrats a d c c nach unten verlängert
werden müssen um die Kopfproportion zu bekommen.

Gegebene Kopflänge 24 cm = b f
4 Teile derselben ergibt 1/4 = a b
Tangentiale a d ergibt Nase
Kugel, Diagonale a h =
Kreisbogen d h ergibt
Stirnkappe
Quadrat a d c c + 1/4 Kopflänge
ergibt a d g f als "Kopffeld"

a = Ohrwurzel
Punkt b Oberende
c c Unterlinie

(5.Sid.)

Type of head

approximately 3 equal parts, the tranquil part, the skull
                              the complicated part, the face
                              the supporting part, the neck

Different forms of head

Forms of face with different features emphasized
all nose
root of nose
all mouth
all chin
all eye

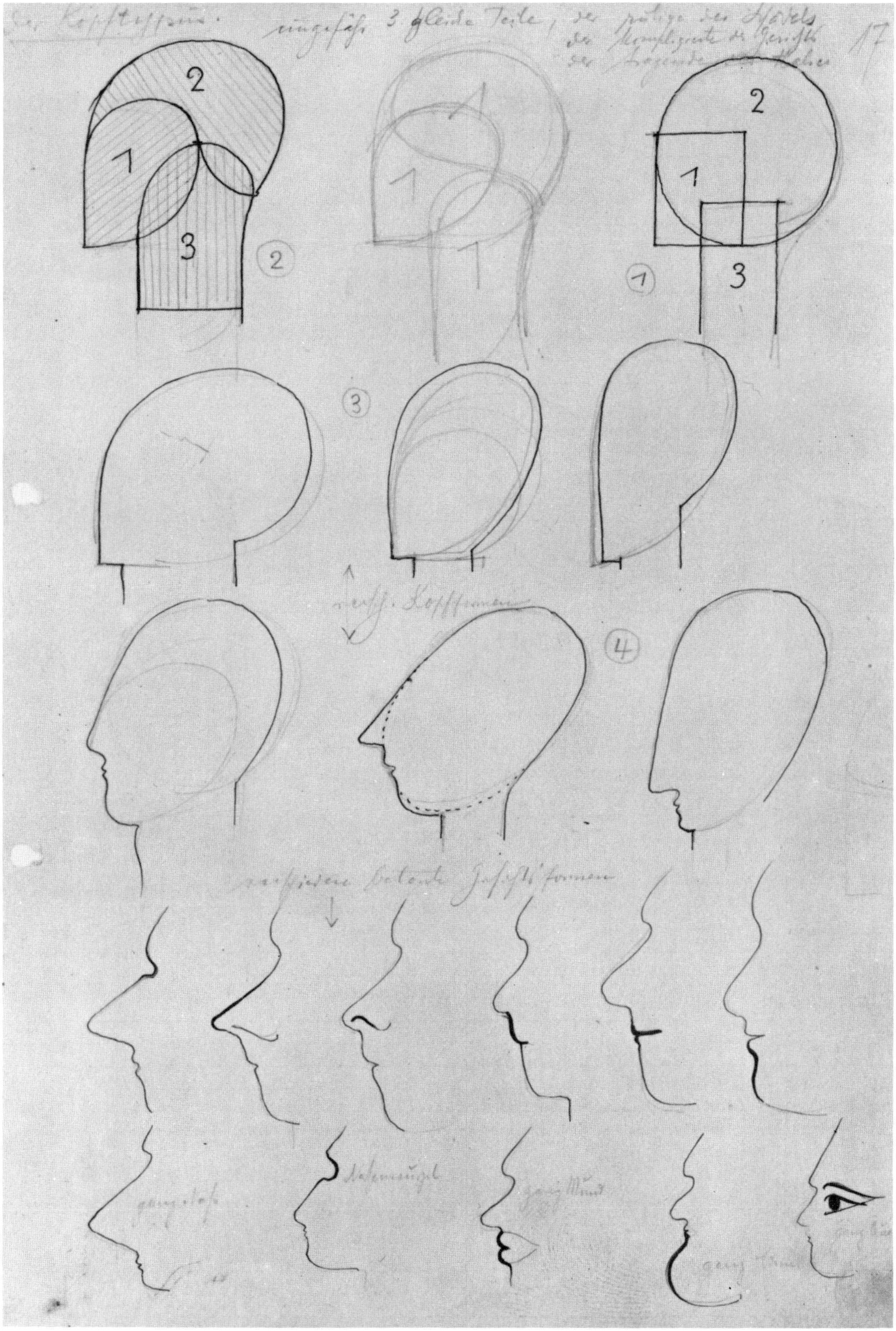

ungefähr 3 gleiche Teile

Natural sciences

As emerges from the syllabus 'Subject of instruction: man' and from Schlemmer's notes for his Bauhaus book, the range of this part of the course was very wide. As a result of his metaphysical systemization (the cosmos as a union of mind, nature and psyche), the fields of natural science and philosophy often overlap. Consideration of matter (nature, the body) begins with the concept of world ether (Ernst Haeckel), proceeds via the atom and the molecule to the cell, to embryology and to the theory of the ectoblast and to the ontogenesis of the internal organs. Human anatomy includes in particular the systems of bones, ligaments and muscles and touches upon veins, nerves, the internal organs and the organs of sense, with special emphasis on the eye and the ear. Much space is devoted to the normal physiology of man, especially the chemical composition of the body and the problems which arise from the upright posture of man. There are in addition a few anthropological comparisons of skulls and a short system of phrenology. There were no notes for the other scientific subjects scheduled in the syllabus beyond those mentioned here.

Bibliography to the chapter on natural science
[After O. Schlemmer]

Buschan, Georg, *Menschenkunde*, Stuttgart 1923.

Bardeleben, Karl von, *Anatomie des Menschen*. Leipzig and
    Berlin 1918/9.

Dubal, Mathias, *Grundriss der plastischen Anatomie*. Stuttgart
    1922.

Frizzi, Ernst, *Anthropologie*. Berlin and Leipzig 1921.

Froriep, August, *Anatomie für Künstler*. Leipzig 1880.

Haeckel, Ernst, *Natur und Mensch*. Leipzig 1920.

Heilborn, Adolf, *Entwicklungsgeschichte des Menschen*. Leipzig
    and Berlin 1914.

Hufeland, Christoph Wilhelm, *Makrobiotik oder die Kunst, das
    menschliche Leben zu verlängern*. Leipzig 1926.

Lehrbuch der systematischen und topographischen Anatomie.
    (Schlemmer gives no author or publisher.)

Lehrbuch der topographischen Anatomie. (Schlemmer gives no
    author or publisher.)

Ostwald, Wilhelm, *Grosse Männer*. Leipzig 1919.

Ranke, Johannes, *Der Mensch*. 1888–90.

Sachs, Heinrich, *Bau und Tätigkeit des menschlichen Körpers*.
    Leipzig and Berlin 1916.

Schider, Fritz, *Plastisch-anatomischer Handatlas*. Leipzig 1902.

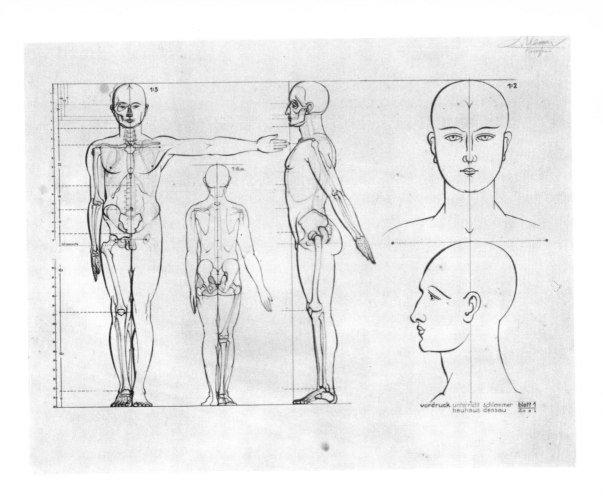

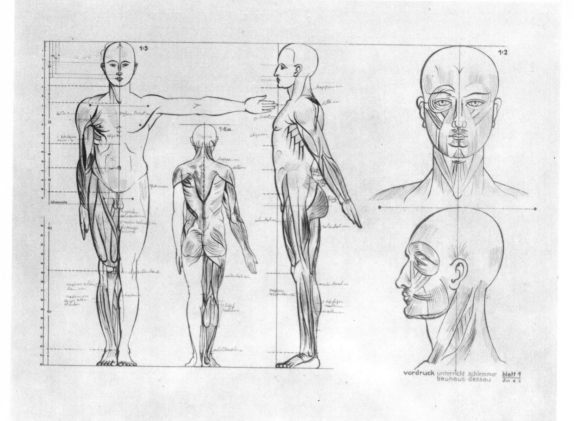

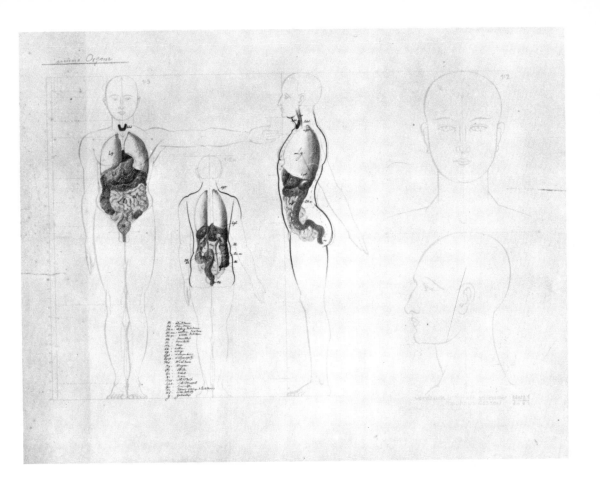

Sound Mechanism

To the nerve cells of the centre of hearing in the cerebrum.

Outer ear free-standing, middle and inner ear embedded in the bony cavities of the skull.

The three semi-circular canals [Bg = Bogengänge] have nothing to do with hearing; they are an organ for the maintenance of balance, of consciousness of the position of the head in space.

The cochlea [Sch = Schnecke] is properly speaking the terminal of the auditory nerves.

The malleus [H = Hammer] with process lies hard against the tympanum [T = Trommelfell]. Its head is secured by an articulation to the anvil.

The anvil [A = Amboss] is attached by a long process to the smallest stapes, the stirrup-bone [St = Steigbügel], by a knob. Its footplate closes the upper fenestra which leads to the labyrinth. This is fastened by a fine membrane to O [fenestra ovalis, closed by a membrane].

The inside of the labyrinth of the ear is covered by a fine thin membrane and this membranous sack is full of fluid. The fluid moves with the oscillations against the tympanum and thence against the stapes. The fluid makes a circuit, twice through the cochlea. The cochlea itself is divided into two. The dividing wall, the membranous plate, carries the ends of the auditory nerves, the so-called organ of Corti. It is a kind of strung key-board, longer towards the bass, shorter towards the treble. Extremely complex inner organism.

(Ornamental gardens of an ear-specialist!)

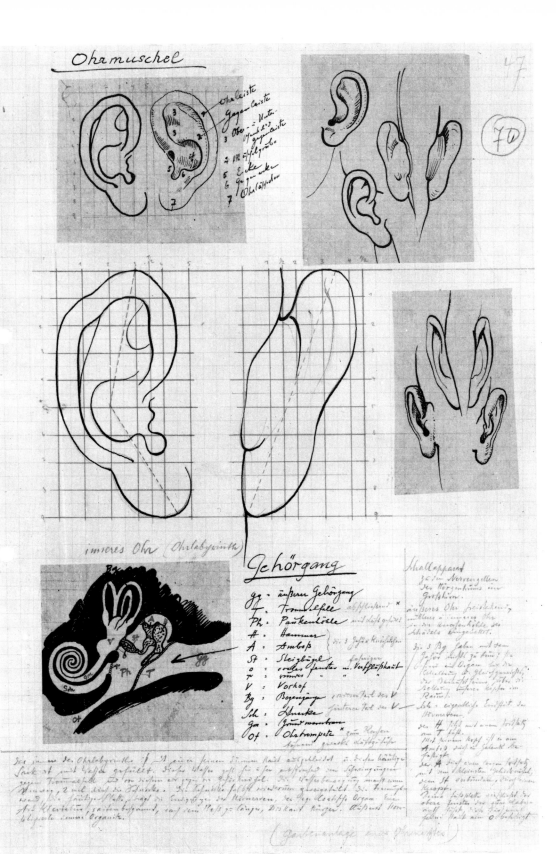

Ohrmuschel

Gehörgang

inneres Ohr (Ohrlabyrinth)

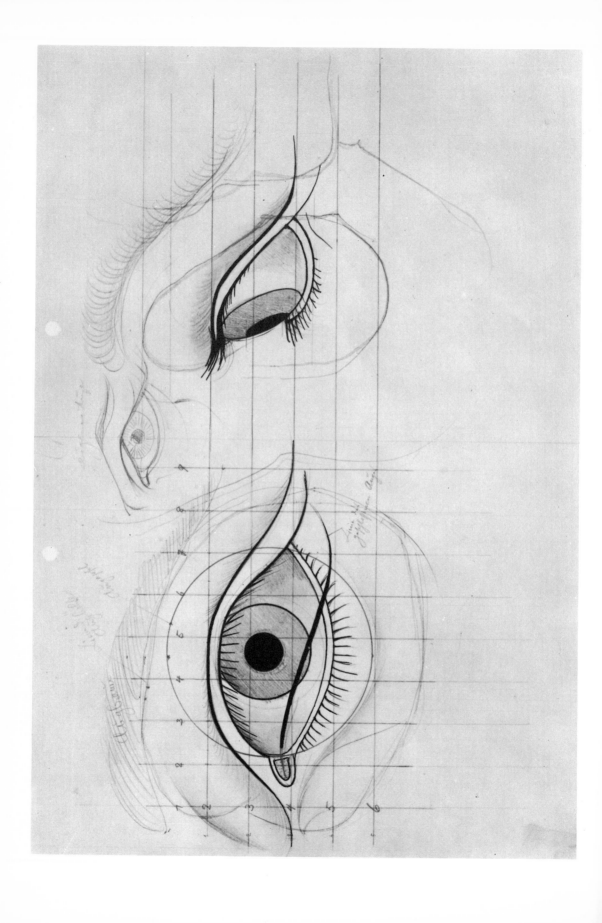

Figure drawing

[1] Oskar Schlemmer, Letter to T., Dessau, 6 October 1927, page 217.

'Schedule of lessons. There is no development course for the advanced fourth semester. I suggested "figure drawing", which fell on fertile ground and was accepted at once. Now presumably I have to give a lesson a week. I should like to work up the subject, which is very much in my line and which the students badly want, into a "compendium of the figural idea".' Schlemmer made this announcement on 6 October 1927[1] and work on the present chapter followed.

In figure drawing Oskar Schlemmer gave the Bauhaus student his formal groundwork for the pictorial representation of the human figure. Whereas the academic aim was to limit this groundwork to the optical drawing of the head and the nude and draped model, Schlemmer took a new line which corresponded both with the tendencies of the Bauhaus and – at least in outline – with the teaching and working methods of the old masters. His organization of this course of study according to the use of 'pure' means – line, plane, chiaroscuro and colour – and the picture space which evolved out of them, ran parallel with Klee's and Kandinsky's teaching. His development of a formal schema for constructing the human figure – the establishment of a formal repertoire – follows the same course as the workshop teaching of the old masters. In this Schlemmer did not proceed from the assumption that an authentic artistic form could be achieved only by constructive means, but certainly from the assumption that it is possible to work out formal approaches from which an up-to-date and personal formal vocabulary could be derived. Like all great masters, Schlemmer knew from personal experience that intuition alone is not enough; if it is to be fruitful and able to evolve to the full, it must be able to command a knowledge and experience of formation and form, and art teaching can prepare the ground for this knowledge and experience.

For this task Schlemmer was able to draw upon certain discoveries by his predecessors and contemporaries, such as those of Cézanne and the Cubists. An entry in a diary of as early as October 1915 indicates that he did so :

the square of the chest,

the circle of the stomach,

cylinders of the arms and lower part of the legs,

spheres of the joints at elbow, knee,

shoulder, joint,

triangle of the nose. [2]

[2] Oskar Schlemmer, Diary, October 1915, page 43.

Like his exemplars in this sort of analysis and reduction of natural forms to geometrical figures, Schlemmer saw that it was possible to obtain simple organizational schemes, the autonomy of which, like the laws governing their assemblage, could be apprehended and could therefore be applied with great consistency. This early, still objective analysis developed into one in which the geometrical figure became supreme. These simple organizational schemes – it is not quite apposite to describe them as 'elementary' – can be reproduced at will and can therefore also be taught. They are a specific foundation for the (imaginary) construction of a human figure and yet are so general and so little binding that individual formulations can be evolved out of them, as is best demonstrated by Schlemmer himself.

With this method Schlemmer won anti-academic ground for figure drawing too : whereas the academies sought to arrive at the concept of a human figure as an artistic form from the outside, from copying a model, Schlemmer's path to such a form starts from the centre of the formal problems of the human figure : in formal analysis of the physical figure, in geometrical reduction of its complex construction and configuration.

As his teaching schedules show, Schlemmer built the theory of proportion and anatomy into his figure drawing. In the interests of clarity the several subjects of instruction were separated.

Figure drawing

(1) **Measurements:** height
     (dimensions)   breadth
                       depth
                       (circumference)
(2) **Form:** (the simplest, normal, elementary, lapidary)
            on the surface
            spatial, plastic   theory of
                                                proportion
(3) **Construction:** calculation of form, proportion; reduction to
                  geometry, measurement, Golden Section etc. (until
                  now linear skeleton, also the spatial (building of
                  constructive people etc.))
(4) **Plasticity** (modelling) surface of the image which is formed by
(5) **Anatomy**
           (a) external: skin, muscles, flesh
           (b) internal: the skeleton, the invisible organs, position, function, special
               feature
(6) **Movement:** possibility of movement, conformity to laws, mechanics, organic system
              (biomechanics)
(7) **Composition:** representation, of one and several figures on the surface, in space,
              static, dynamic, functional
(8) **The ideal type:** comparative art history, (photographs 'which is the most
              handsome?')

- -

(1) head: (a) hair, (b) skull, (c) nose, (d) eye, (e) mouth, (f) chin, (g) ear
      (physiognomical studies, study of character, theory of race)
(2) neck: larynx, vertebra
(3) trunk: (a) breast, (b) back, (c) stomach, (d) buttocks
(4) legs: (a) thigh, (b) knee, (c) lower leg, (d) foot (joint, heels, toes)
(5) arms: (a) upper arm, (b) elbow, (c) forearm
(6) hand: wrist, palm (chiromancy), fingers (prints)

Course of instruction:

	(1) **Schematic drawing**
	Theory
with	(2) **Applied drawing**
	Practice from plaster or live model
lastly	(3) **Free composition**
	Application of theory and practice

(1) Schematic drawing

Fig. Draw. page 1

(I) . . . to draw: (a) the **whole rhythmic line** of a body
curved undulating line

(b) **straight lines,** curved lines transformed
into straight lines, which, however, are then
only partly

(c) the **axes** of the human body.
establish these.

(d) next to the axes, the **exterior, plastic** lines
which model the body. Then also

(e) all the **sections** along the axes, horizontal
and vertical.

(II) Measurement

1. **Normal measurement**
   (a1) length of head
   (a2) unit of spinal column
2. **Key to proportion** according to C. Schmidt
3. **The module** according to Carus
4. **The Golden Section**
5. Dürer's measurement
6. Dürer's and Leonardo's circles
7. [?] square O.S.
8. Type and modelling
9. Measurement according to Dürer, division into 1, 2, 3, 4 parts etc.
10. Dürer's figure, reduced to straight lines
11. (a) front and profile contrasted
    (b) box perspective
    (c) tracing of Dürer's sections
    (d) these transferred to the box figure

1 Normal measurement
2 Length of head – spinal column
3 Key to proportion
4 Module
5 Golden Section
6 Dürer's circle – Leonardo
7 [?] square
8 Type and modelling
9 Measurement – Dürer
10 Dürer's figure in straight lines
11 a, b, c, d

Wintersemester 31/32

L E H R G A N G:

    1) S c h e m a t i s c h e s Z e i c h n e n
    Theorie

nebe1 : 2) A n g e w a n d t e s Z e i c h n e n
    Praxis / nach Modell in Gips oder Leben

zuletzt: 3) F r e i e K o m p o s i t i o n
    Anwendung von Theorie und Praxis

1) S c h e m a t i s c h e s Z e i c h n e n

Fig.Zch.Seite 1 -

I).......zu zeichnen: a) die gesamtrythmische Linie eines Körpers
    gebogene,geschwungene Linie

    b) die G e r a d e n , jene in gerade umge-
    wandelt,welche jedoch dann nur z.T. die

    c) die A c h s e n des menschl.Körpers sind.
    diese feststellen.

    d) als nächstes zu den Achsen,die a u s s e n
    p l a s t i s c h e n Linien,welche den
    Körper modellieren. Ferner ebenso

    e) alle D u r c h s c h n i t t e entlang
    den Achsen,horizontal und vertikal

II) D.i.e..M.a.s.s e: a) das N o r m a l m a s s
    a¹) kopflänge   a²) Wirbelsäulencentat.

    X 2) der P r o p o t i o n s s c h l ü s s e l
    nach C.Schmidt

    X 3) das M o d u l nach Carus

    X 4) der G o l d e n e S c h n i t t

    X 5) die Messung Dürers

    X 6 Kreislinien Dürer & Lonardo

    7 Konvexe Virech ? OS

    8 Typ - Modelling

    9 Maße nach Dürer, Teilung 1,2,3,4 fr.1 :/.

    10 Dürerfigur, gradlinig eingeteilt

    11 a) Vorn - Seite ansicht gegeneinder gestellt
    b) Kartei perspektive
    c) Pan. d'Anenfpeite - Dürer
    d) vom Überlegung - die Kartikylae.

[left margin handwritten notes:]
Normalmaße
kopflänge Wirbelsäule
Proportionsschl.
- modul
gold. schn. Dürer Lion
6 kreislinien Virech
7 konvexe Virech
8 Typ - Modell
   nähe - Dürer
9 Dürerfig, gradlinig
5 blätter
10   a.b.c.d
11

Linear figures

Because it can be modulated, the line is a means of artistic expression. It appears as contour, framework and axis. With his planned use of specific lineations in figure drawing, Schlemmer is systematically linked with the old masters. They originally built up the outlines of the human figure with convex curves, only later and more rarely using both concave and convex curves. Schlemmer, who, as a dancer, had a strong sense of rhythm, liked to use alternating concave and convex curves for the contours of his figures. He also used straight lines in static and dynamic figures.

1. **To draw a figure objectively**
(Test of capacity, individuality etc.)

2. The **simplest linear form** of a human figure
(a) a perpendicular line in relation to surroundings
(b) the letter i
(c) action through undulation
(d) straight line with slight movement can create illusion
(e) intensified by pressure (practice)
(f) the figure with the verticals as strongly maintained as possible
General comment on c–e : the magic power of the simple line

What **further lines or forms** are needed before we can say : this is a human
figure?
(a) the cross
(b) and (c) symbols
(d–f) attempts to form a head
(g) the decisive step = separation of the oblique lines of the legs, slant of the
    line of the head.

1) <u>Unvoreingenommen eine Figur zu zeichnen</u>
(Prüfung auf Fähigkeit, Individuelles, u.s.w.)

2) Die <u>einfachste lineare Form</u> einer menschlichen Figur.
a) Gegenüber der Umwelt eine senkrechte Linie

b) der Buchstabe i

c) Aktion durch Schwung

d) Plastizitätsfähigkeit des leicht bewegten Geraden

e) durch Druck interpretiert (Übungen)

f) Die Figur unter größtmöglichster Wahrung der Senkrechten

allgemein zu c - e : die magische Kraft der einfachen Linie

Welche weiteren Linien oder Formen sind nötig, um Figur zu bestimmen : daß ist eine menschliche Figur :

a) der König
b-c) Zeichen

d-f) Versuche zu Kopfstellungen

g) Das entscheidende Verhältnis u. Abhängigkeit der Beinstellung u. Neigung der Kopflinie

These straight-line figures can suggest life and action

(Bases for a dance notation)
(associative faculty; creative vision!)

(a) parallelism of head and arms
(b) legs straddled
(c) knee bent, gestures of the arms
(d) shoulders slanting
(e) shoulders slanting acutely
(f) tragic pose
(g) trunk slanting
(h) strong deflection so that functional lines come close together
(i) variation on slanting trunk

2

Lebent- und Aktionsfähigkeit solcher Figuren: zweizeiliger
(Grundlagen für eine Tanzschrift)*

a) Parallelität von Kopf- Armen.   b) Beinspreizen.   c) KnicKnick, Armgesta.

d) Schulterschräge   e) starke Schulterschräge   f) tragische Pose

* (des Assoziationsvermögen; die bildende Nachkraft!)

g) Rumpfschräge   h) starke Abbiegung bis Annäherung der Symbolismus binden

i) variierte Kampf-schräge.

Recourse to the **curved line** (gracefulness!)

Combinations of straight and curved lines

Composition of corresponding figures
and so on

[bottom right]
Perspectives or foreshortening front and back

Zuhilfenahme der gebogenen Linie. (Grazie!)

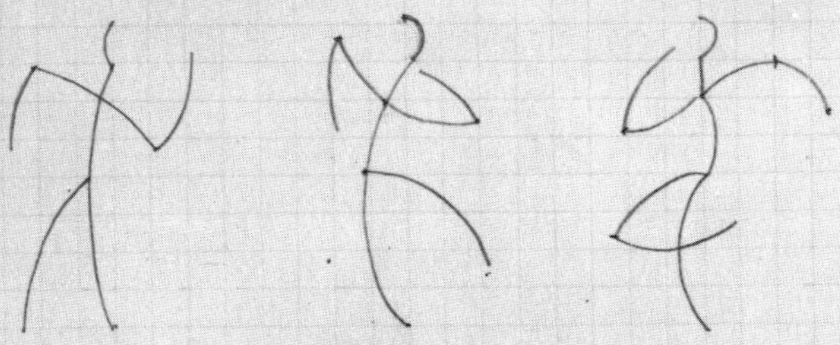

Kombinationen aus geraden und gebogenen Linien

Komposition korrespondirender figuren.

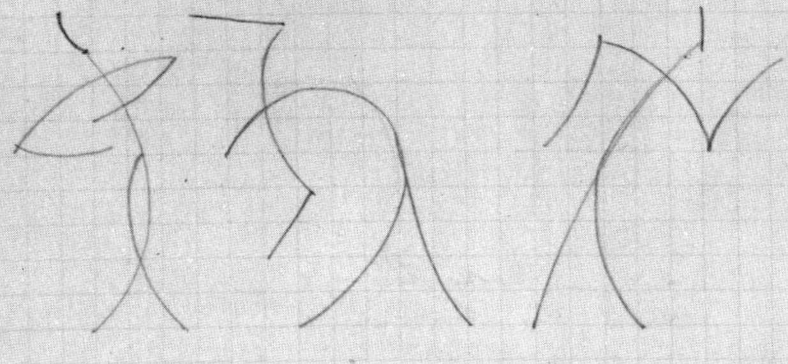

und

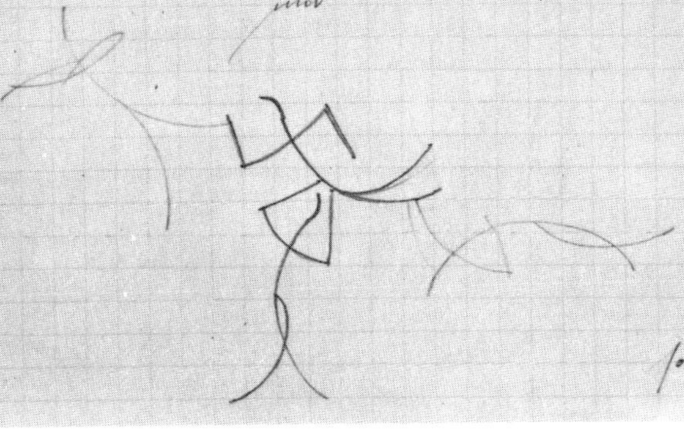

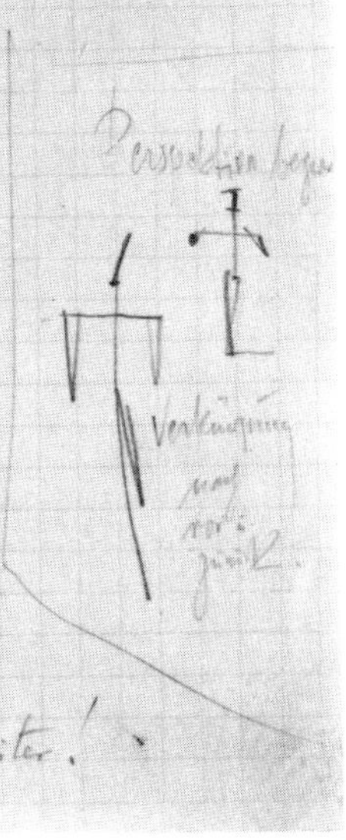

so weiter!

Perspektivisch begon...

Verkürzung nach vor... zurück

First Problem

to draw a human figure, without model, from imagination
so : subjective expression of the concept of man the individual

1. Form, 2. form : expressional power of the simple line
I. From the model (plaster or live)
   Discover the inner structure, the **scaffolding lines**
   around which everything else is built
   differentiated if need be into
   (a) main scaffolding lines
   (b) subsidiary scaffolding lines
   (c) external contour
Geometry : black   main scaffolding of the given information
          red
               } auxiliary lines of the desired figure
          blue
1. Schematic drawing – theory
with
2. practical drawing – from model
3. free composition – combination

1. Aufgabe   eine menschliche Figur zu zeichnen
ohne Modell   nach der Vorstellung
also   zeichnerischer Niederschlag des Begriffs vom
individuellen Mensch.

1. form   2 form

I. Nach dem Modell

Geometrie:

1. Schematisches Zeichnen
theorie
neben

2. praktisches Zeichnen
nach Vorbild

3. freie Komposition

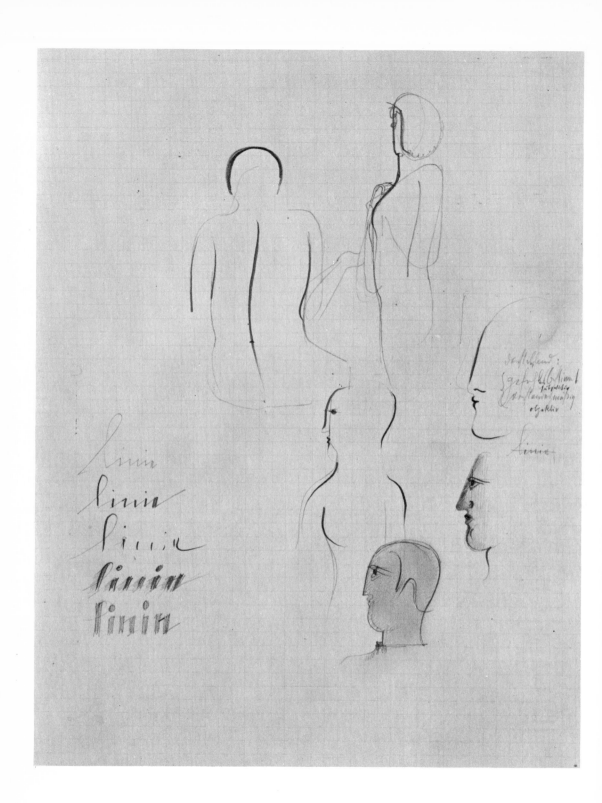

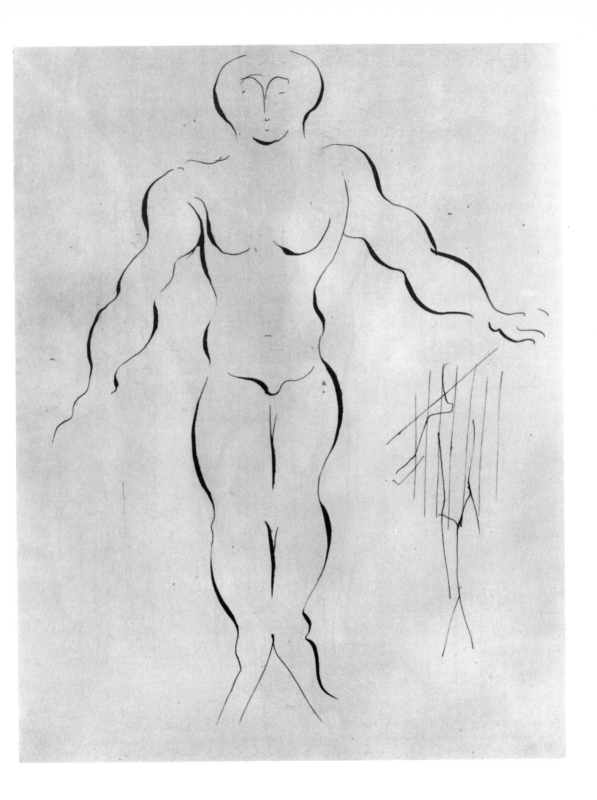

95

Plane and spatial schemata

Circle, square, rectangle, triangle, ellipse and the elements derived from these figures form the material for two-dimensional constructions.

After Dürer's example – and that of the Italian Mannerists – a 'box man' was built out of cubes, as a way of working out the spatial solidity of the figure. Formal schemata constructed of cylinders and spheres have the same purpose. Marked sections and figures broken down into sections give spatial views and show the relationship between contour and solidity (see also instructional plate 11 in section on theory of measurement and proportion). Solidity can also be achieved by chiaroscuro hatching. Chiaroscuro and certain colour contrasts free the figure from the picture plane and create pictorial space. In a two-dimensional pictorial solution a formal relationship between figure and picture plane can be created in the same way (the 'ornament which takes shape between the body and the exterior world').

Need to fix the head distinctly
How?

A circle for head matches the simplicity of the unadorned line
3 dots are enough to characterize it as such

The main divisions and measurements of the body

1. **Longitudinal** divisions
Centre of the body clearly marked by the beginning of the fork of the legs
Head
Collar-bone
Centre of the body
Knee
Foot
Only the 3 main measurements (from collar-bone to end of head uncertain).

Normal measurement 7 head lengths (to be exact: $7\frac{1}{3}$)

Bedürfnis, den Kopf besonders zu fixieren.
Wie?

der Simplizität der einfachen
Linie entspricht der Kreis
als Kopf.

3 Punkte genügen, ihn
als solchen zu charakteri-
sieren.

die Hauptteilungen und Maße des Körpers.

1.) die Längenteilungen

Körper-Mitte, augenfällig
markiert durch
den Beginn
der Beinteilung.

Kopf

Achselhöhlen

Körpermitte

Knie

Fuß

die 3 Hauptmaße schließband
(vom Scheitelbein bis Kopfende unbestimmt)

Normalmaß ⑦ Kopflängen. (genau: 7 ⅓)

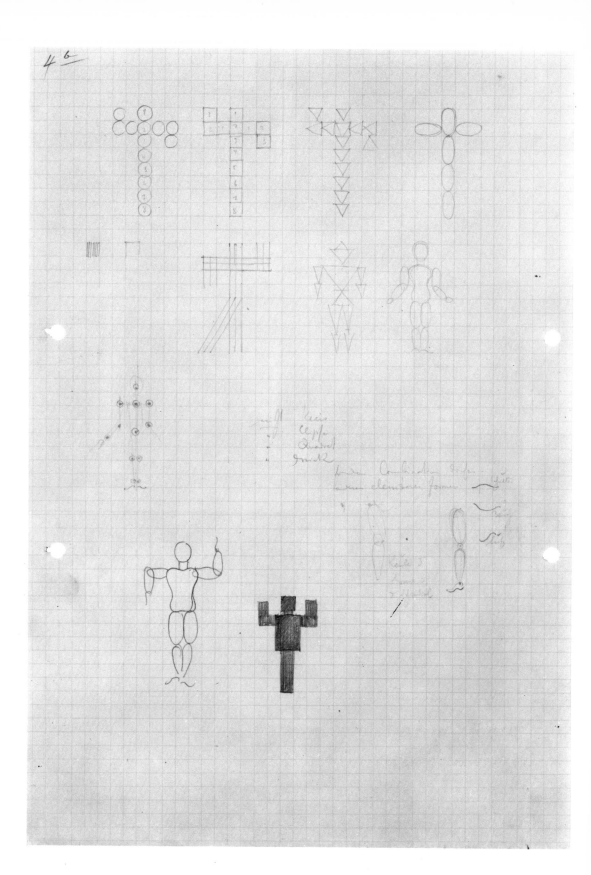

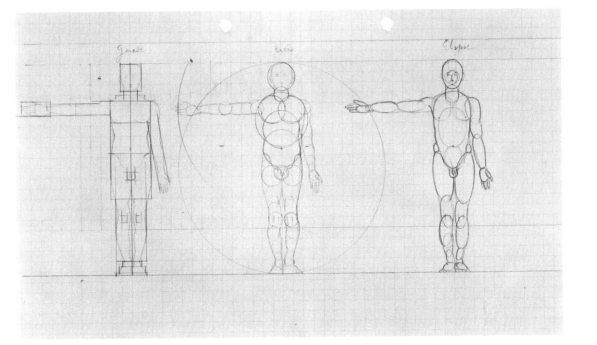

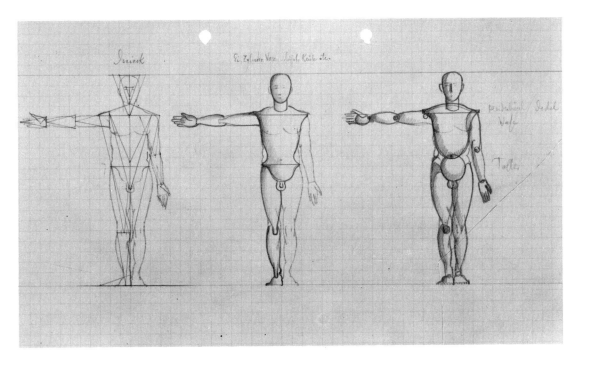

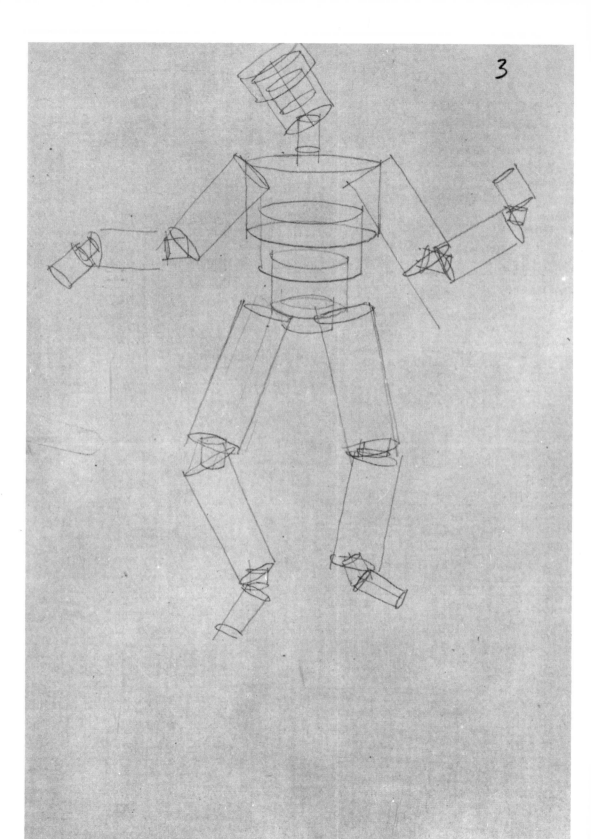

3

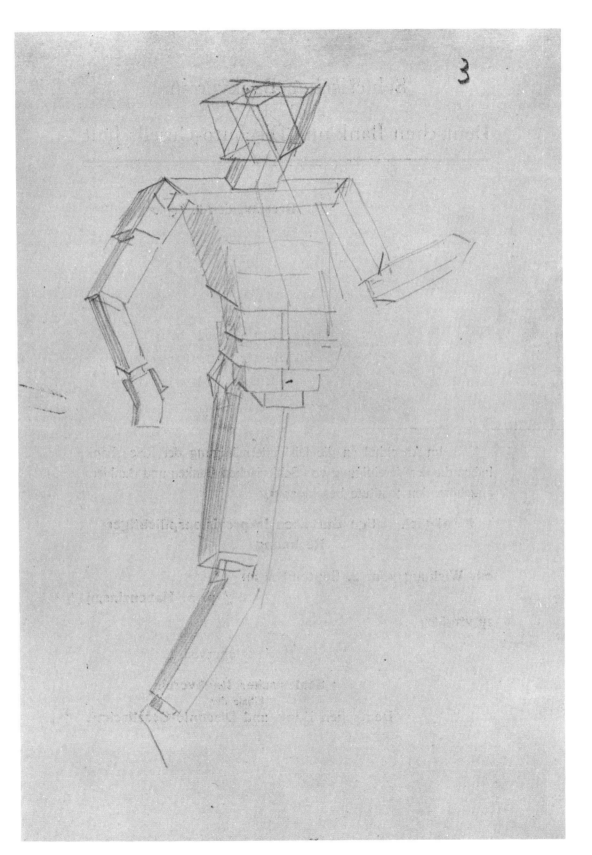

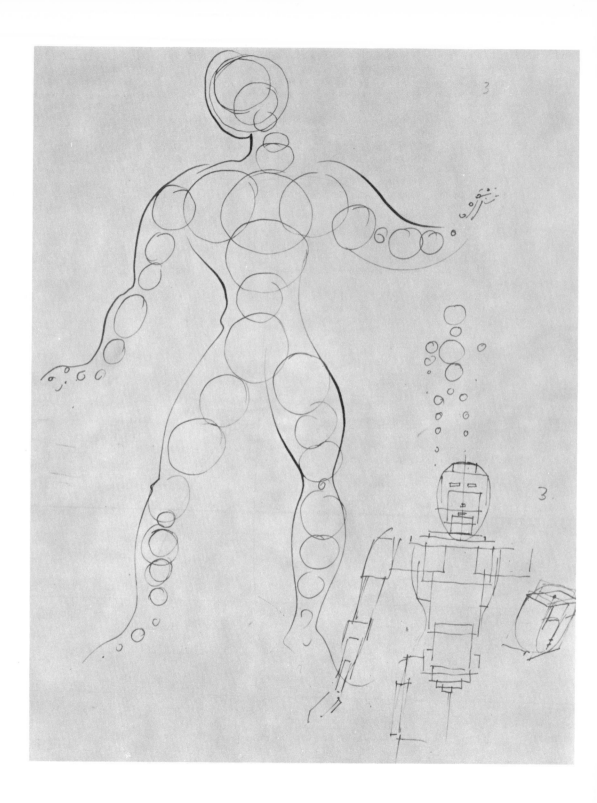

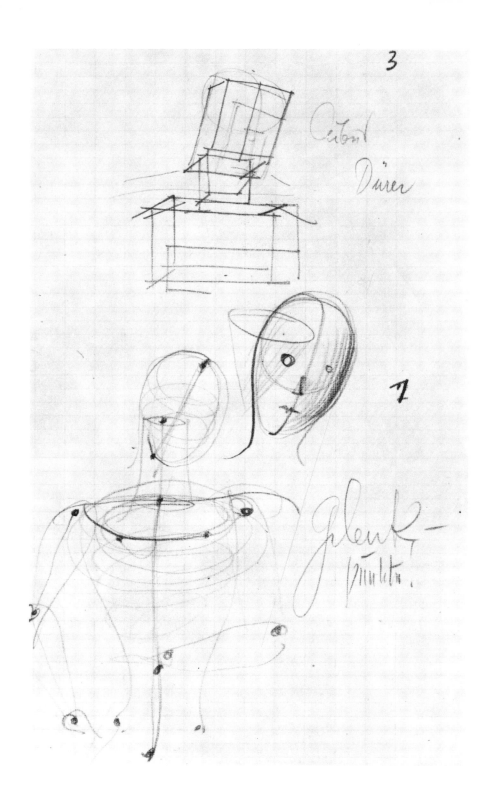

3

Albert
Dürer

1

Gelenk-
punkte.

105

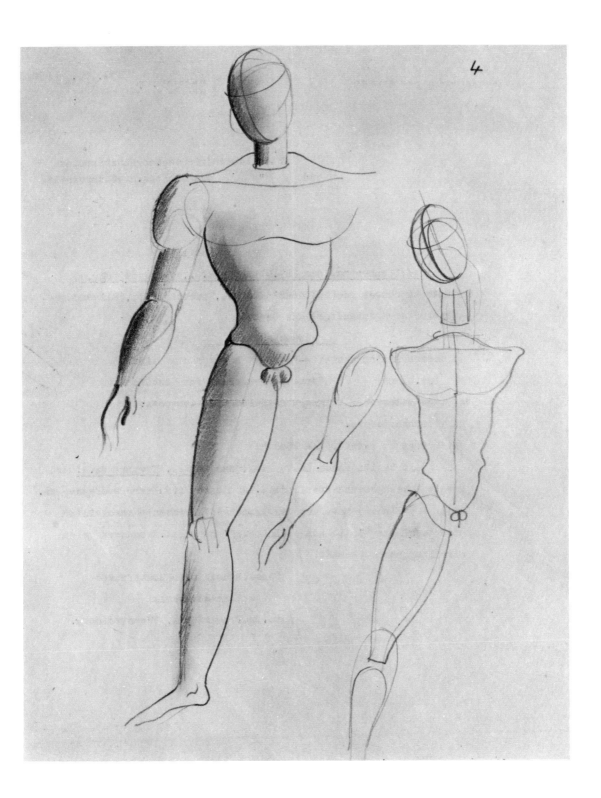

4

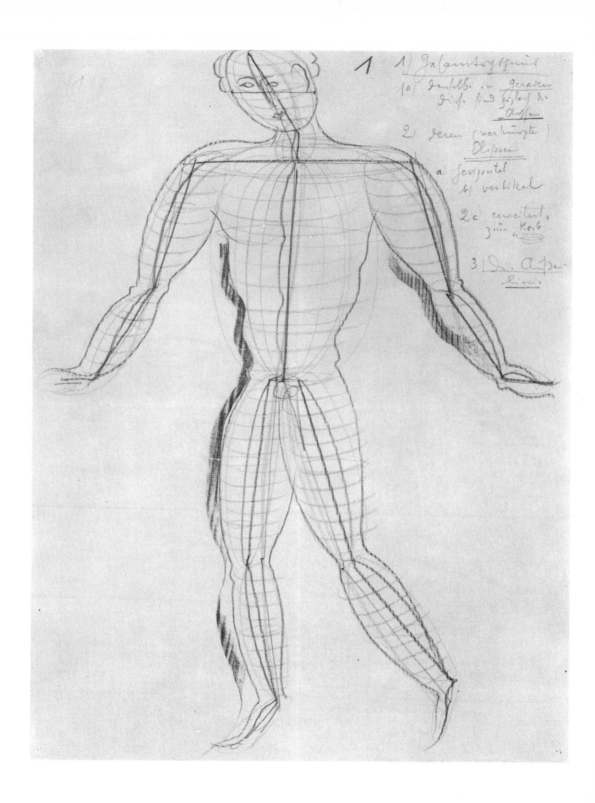

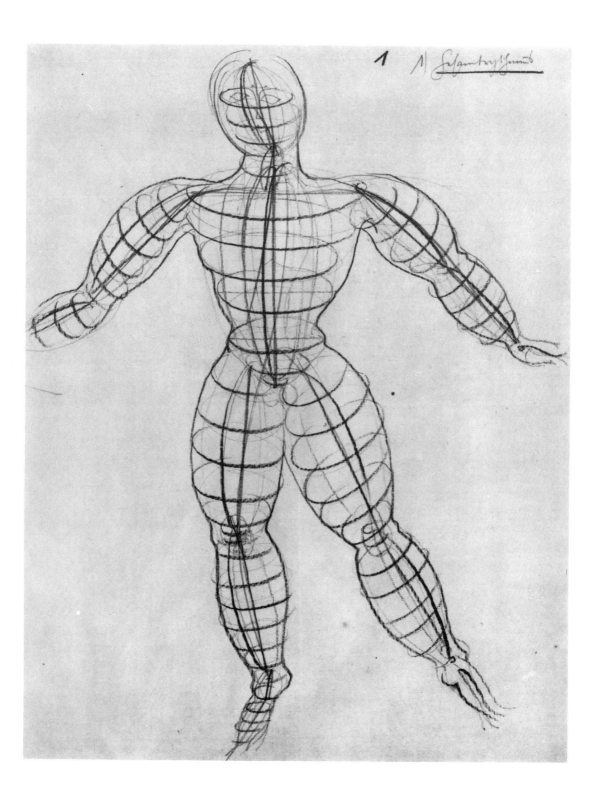

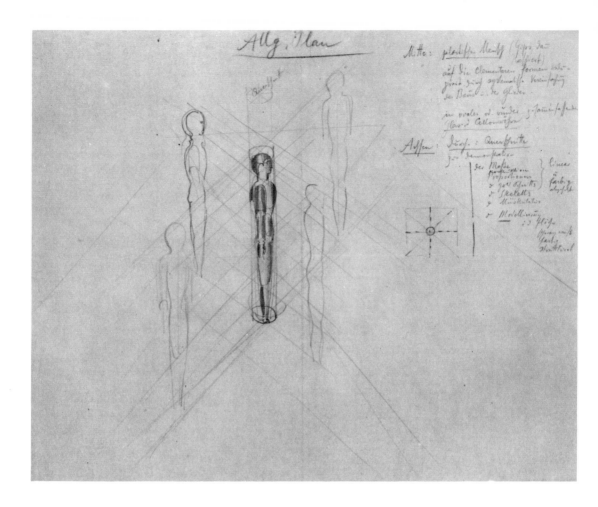

General plan

Centre:
Plastic man (plaster of Paris, laminated), reduced to the elementary forms by systematic simplification of the structure and the limbs in oval or round enclosing **glass or celluloid tube.**

Axes:
Vertical and cross sections for demonstration of

measurement ⎫
construction ⎬ expressed
proportions ⎬ in colour
Golden Section ⎭ and line
skeleton
musculature
modelling
   on the surface
   black and white
   coloured
   structural

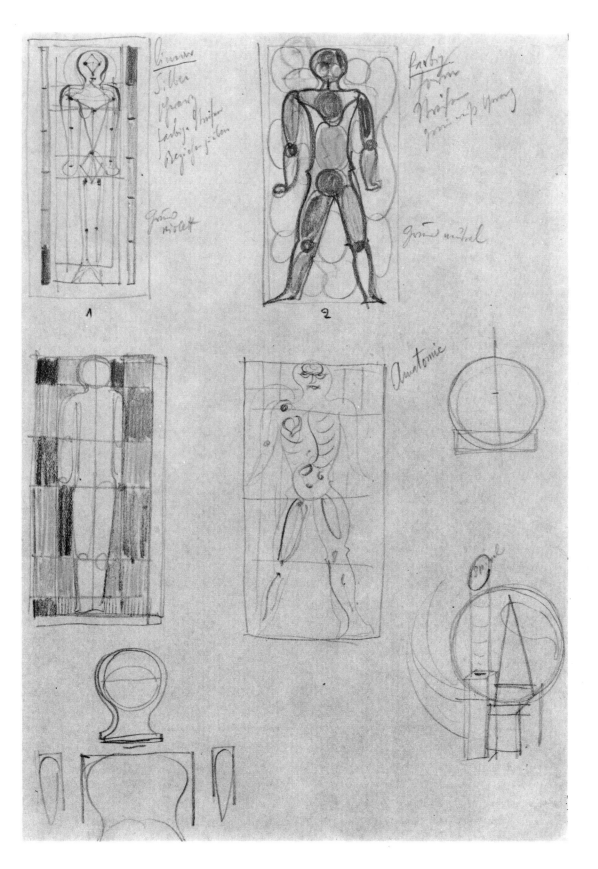

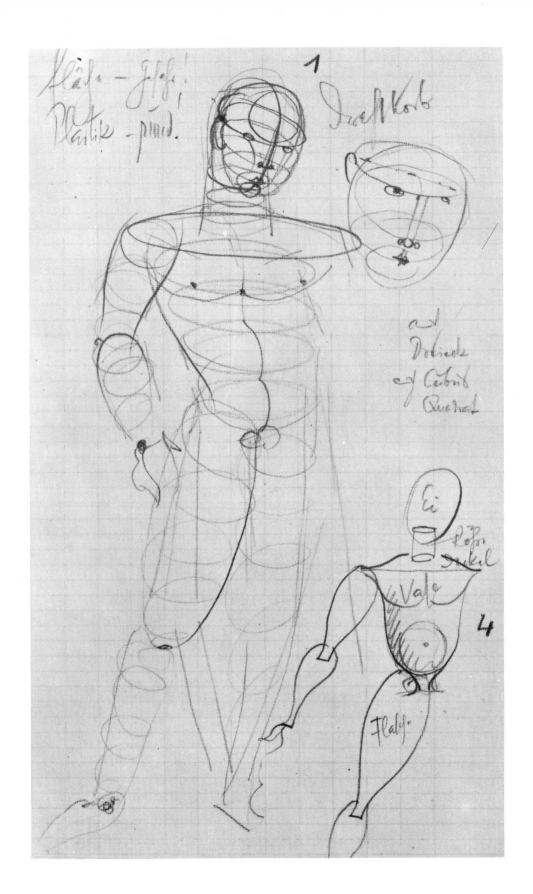

112

The moving figure

The natural movement of man is raised in the dance to a form of artistic expression; but it too is subject to physical laws. When the creative artist constructs the motifs of the movements of his figures by rhythm alone, he replaces physical laws with formal ones. Schlemmer's line-figures — especially those formed of circular lines — show a consistent rhythmic movement. As a dancer, Schlemmer was most actively concerned with the body in movement, and much space is therefore devoted to the figure in movement in his notes on figure drawing; it pervades all his figure drawing and is made a special subject as well.

Rhythm is the system of organization which in the visual arts makes transient events simultaneous and thereby visually intelligible: the artist alternates and repeats the contrary and parallel movements of a figure and a motif of movement is implied. This purely rhythmic manner of representation receives its own dynamic from movement.

The head can bend while the upper part of the body remains rigid
The trunk, the arm, can bend

Plastic shading
(a) from the left
(b) from the right

Illustration of all the movement that can be made from a standing position
(= model)
   of the head
   of the trunk
   of the arms   upper arm, forearm
   of the legs   thigh, lower leg
   of the feet
the maximum of every movement much accentuated

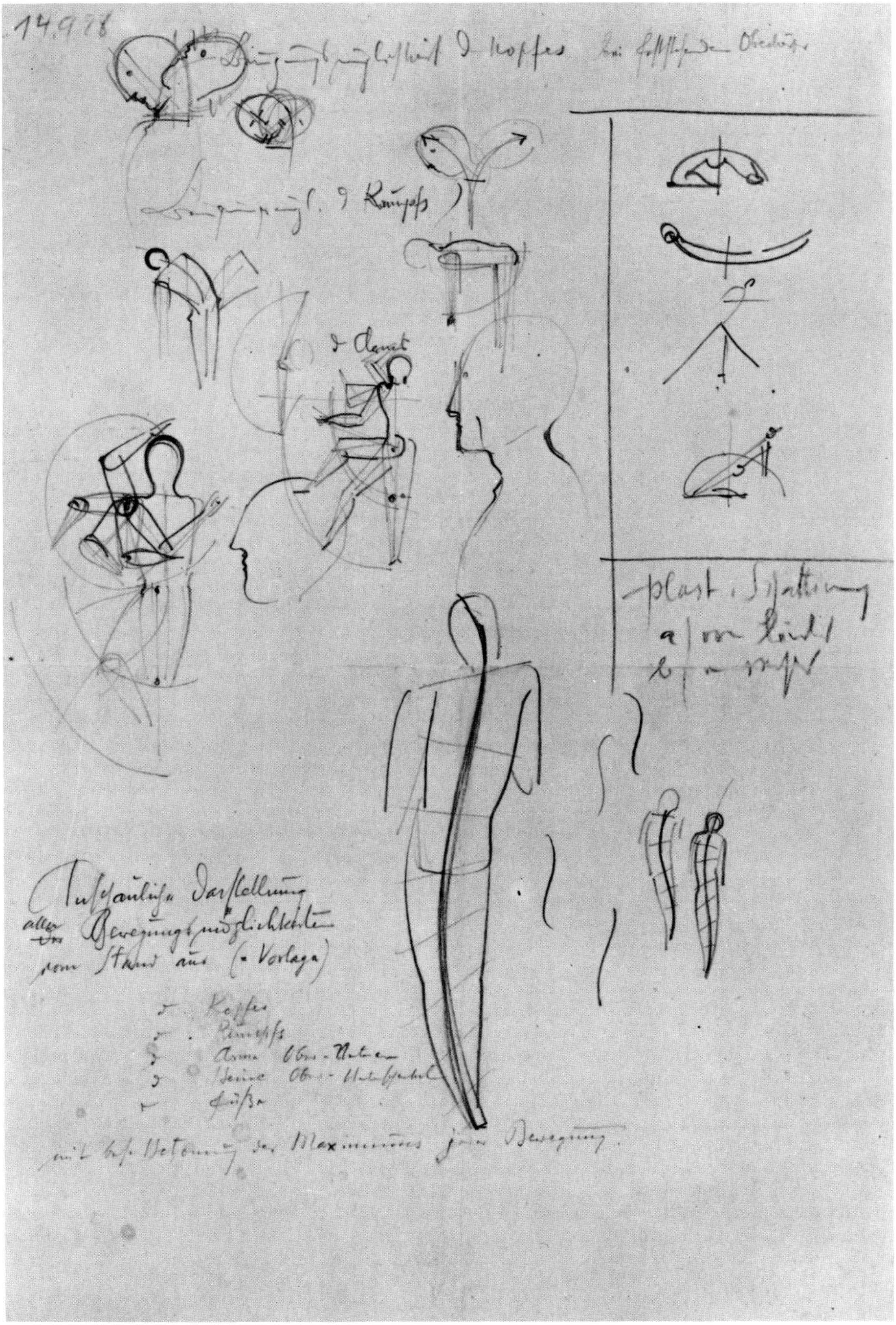

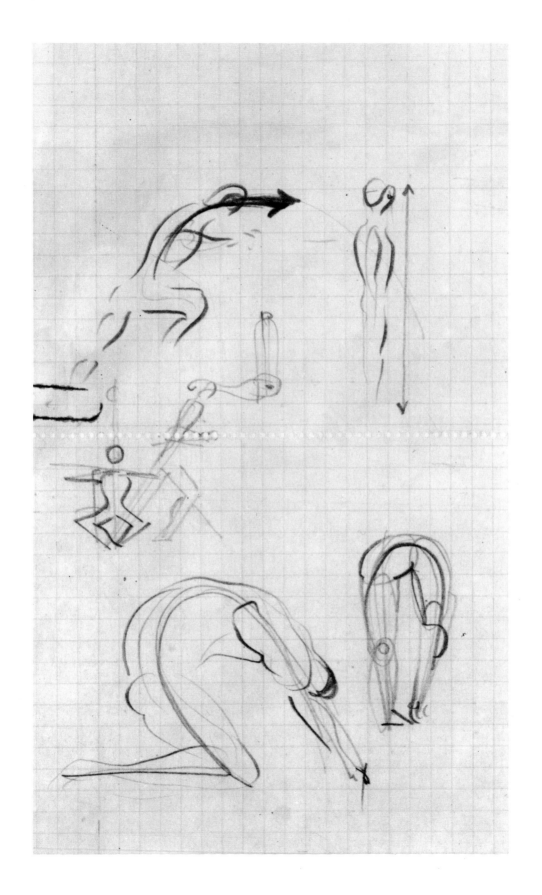

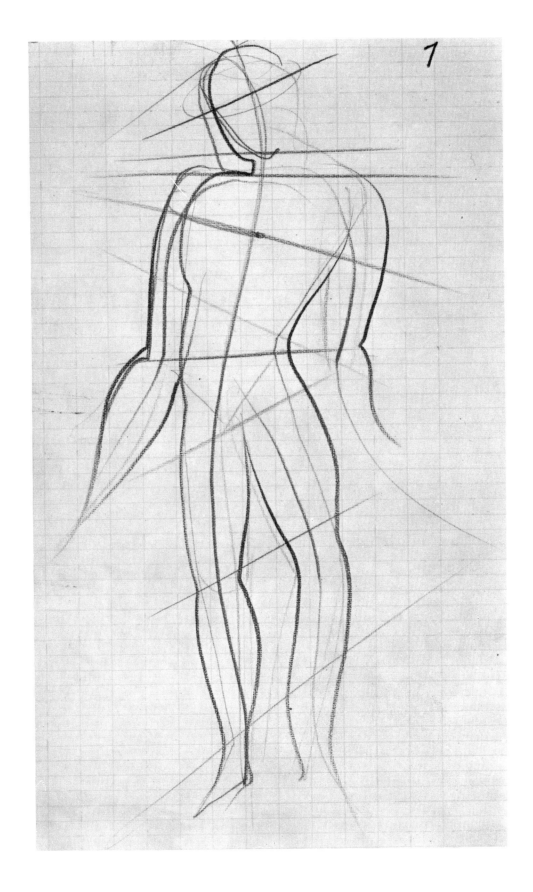

Things it would be desirable to do:

(a) drawing of the points of contact [?] with the world around us
(b) drawing of lines of feeling with the eyes closed (how do I see my body?)

Feeling in a narrow space
Feeling in a large space
Space: 5 minutes long
       10 minutes wide
        3 minutes deep
      (minutes = metres)

Relationship with pieces of furniture, their character with regard to the body (measurement and movement)
Table for stout draughtsmen [?] distance they can reach, distance they can bend etc.

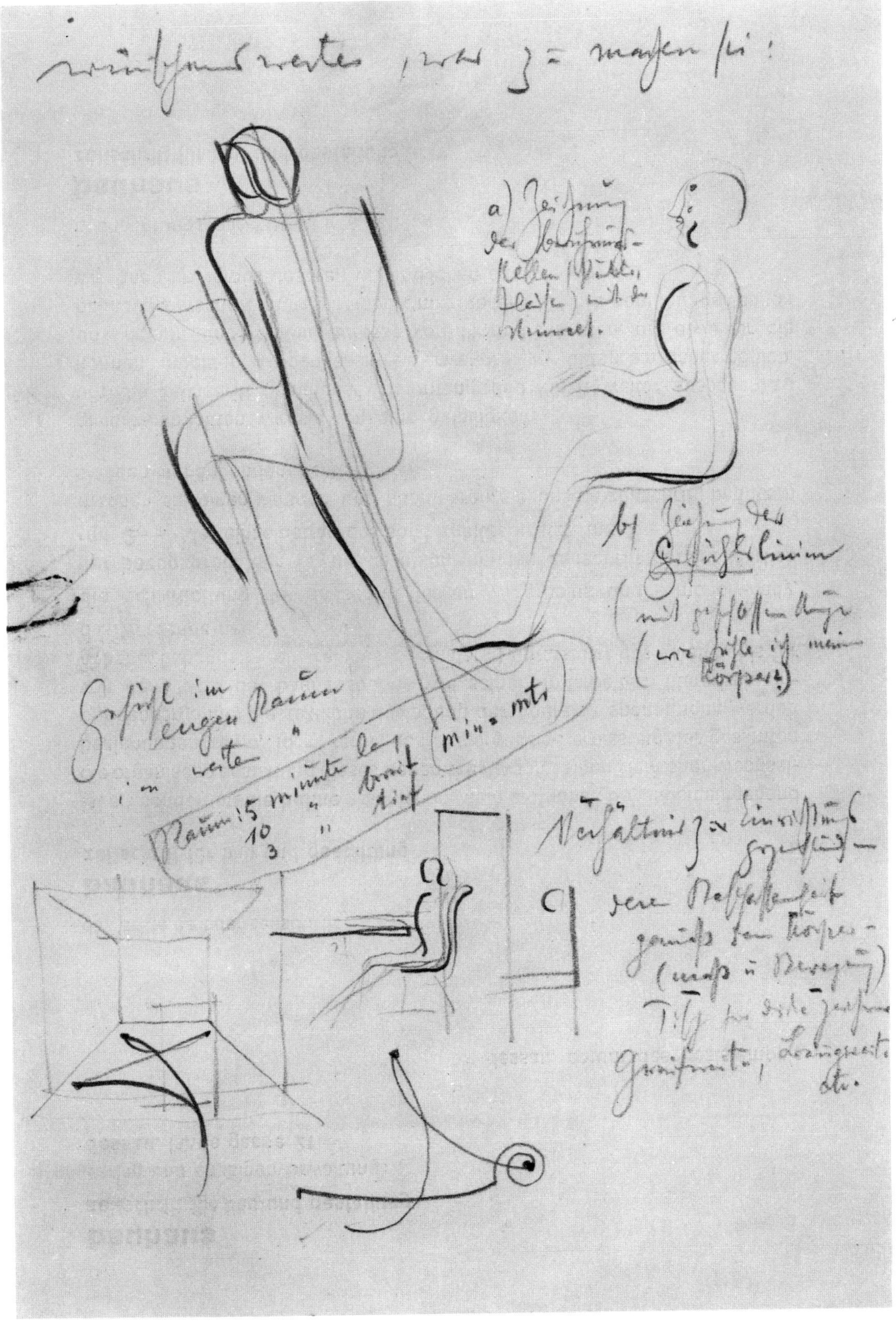

a) Zeichnung der Kontaktstellen (Stuhl, Fläche) mit der Umwelt.
b) Zeichnung der Gefühlslinien (mit geschlossenen Augen) (wie fühle ich meinen Körper)
Gefühl im engen Raum
im weiten "
Raum: 5 minute lang
10 " breit
3 " tief
Verhältnis zu Einrichtungsgegenstände
etc.

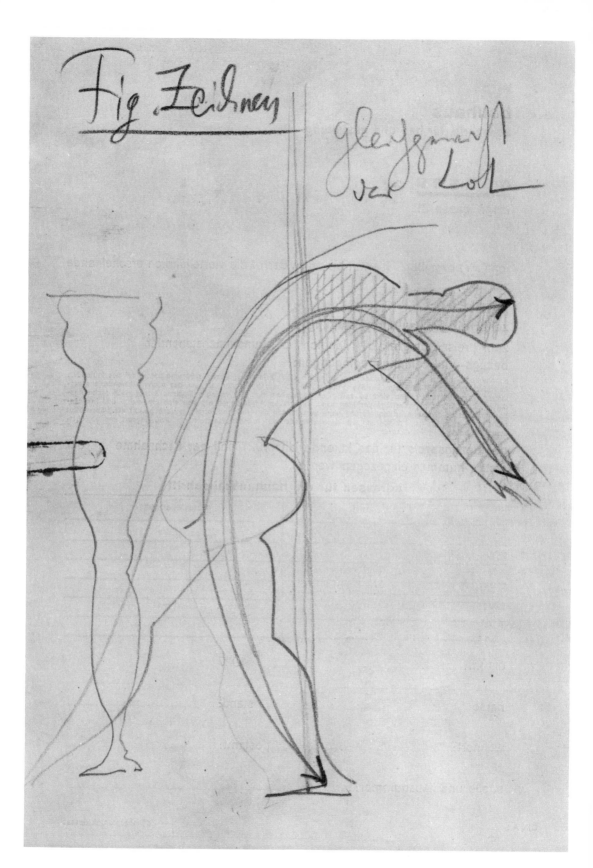

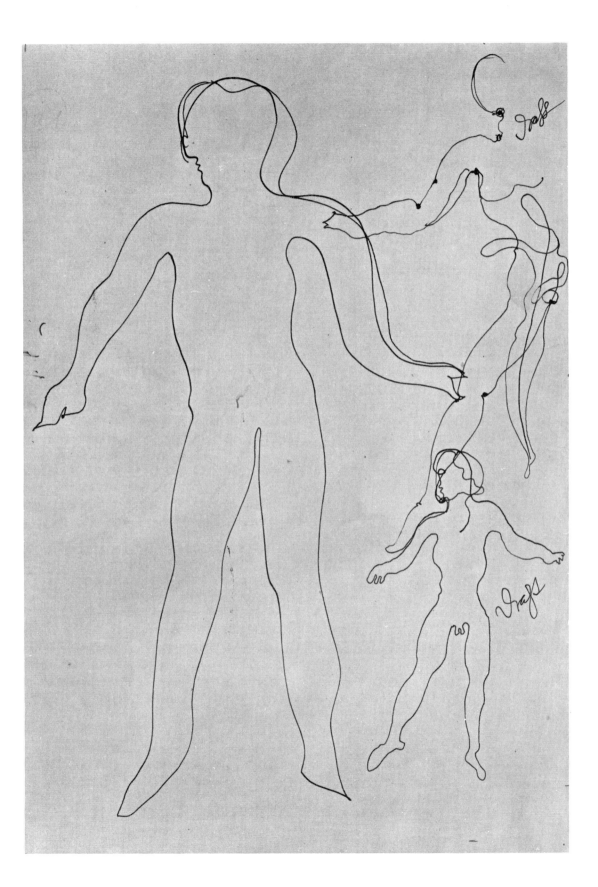

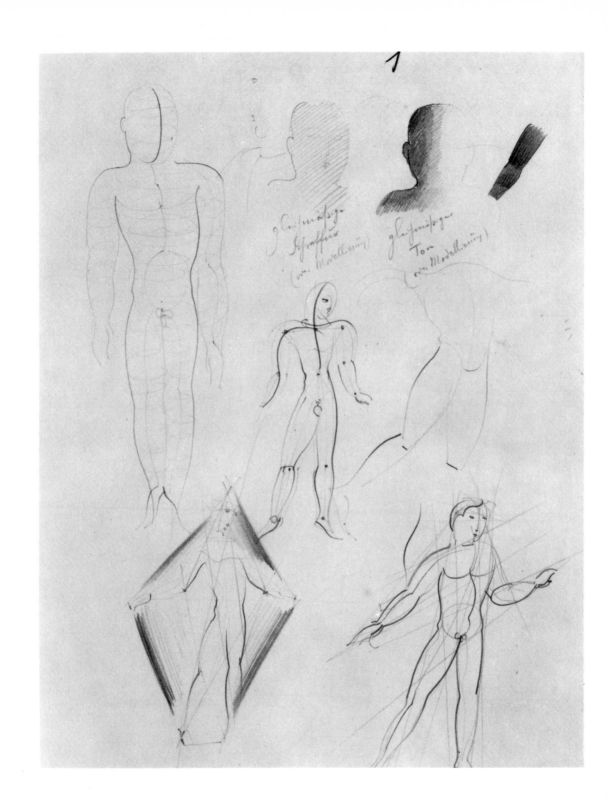

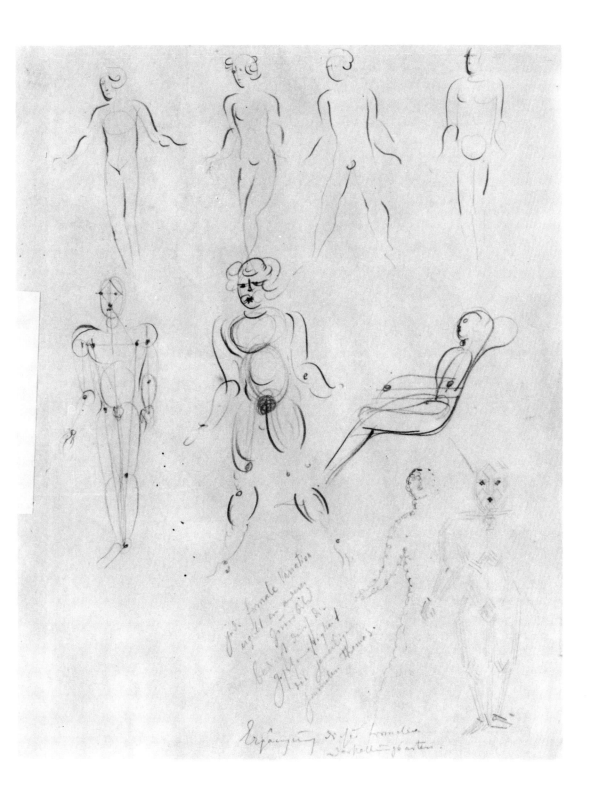

The figure in space

The figure conceived in space brings up the question of the
relationship figure – picture-plane – picture-space. Since a self-
contained figure has a tendency to detach itself from the picture-
plane, this presents the artist with the task of creating a relationship between a spatial figure and the spatial arrangements of the
picture-plane. Particularly in his paintings, Schlemmer evolved
two-dimensional arrangements out of the axes of the figures or
brought the spatial figures into the system of axes of the picture
space.

Only two sheets of the notes for this book are devoted to this
difficult problem.

Schlemmer's plane and spatial prospects contain architectonic
motifs which are presented orthogonally or in exaggerated per-
spective. The opportunity denied to Schlemmer on a large scale –
to collaborate as a painter in architectural projects, like the builders
of the lodges – he experienced on a small scale in his easel-
painting, where he fused architecture and figure into a visual unity.

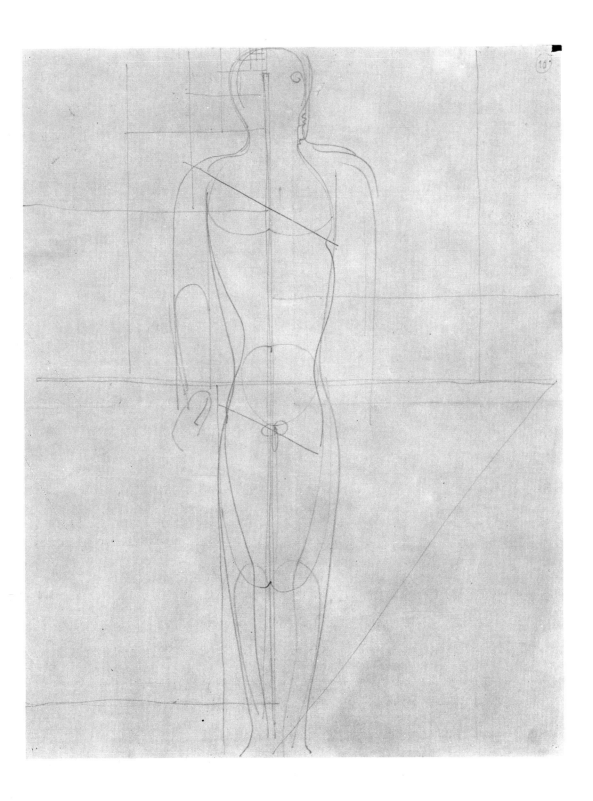

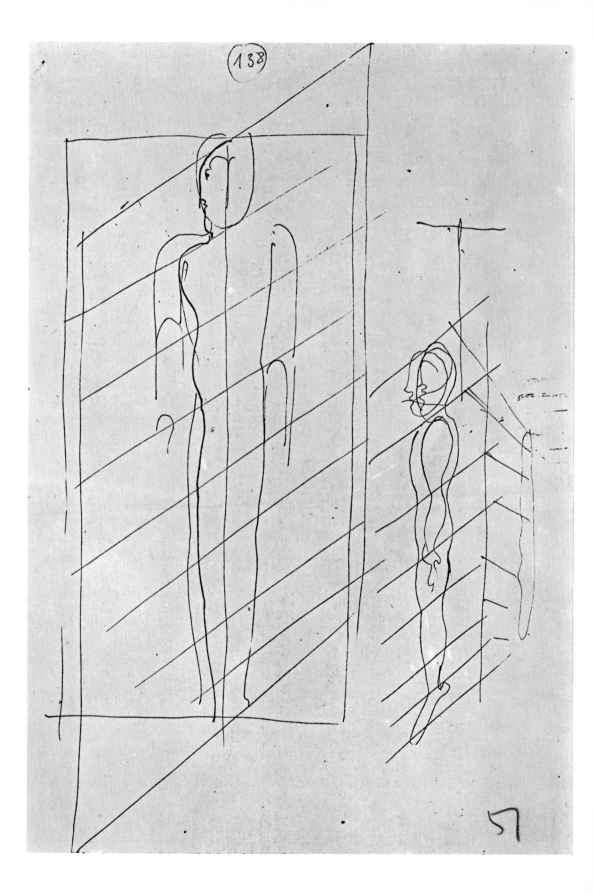

Stylistic analyses

The course 'man' also provided for analysis of figural representations by old or modern masters. There are only two sheets of these
analyses. The sheet carrying many figures must have served merely
as an aid to Schlemmer's memory, for on it he has graphically
sketched such abstract stylistic features as the vertical extension
of the Gothic, the diagonal movement of the Baroque and such-
like. The diagram after Juan Gris's *Seated Woman* demonstrates
in an analytic way the use of straight and curved lines and the
embedding of the figure with parallel lines (planes) in the picture-
plane.

With this kind of pictorial analysis Schlemmer was entering upon
a path which can lead to the discovery of formal rules in the
creative arts, since principles of form are elucidated (formal value
– contrary formal value – combining formal value; contrast and
resolution of the contrasts; insertion of specific figures into the
picture-plane; relation of the components of the picture to one
another and to the picture-plane. Schlemmer also analyzed his
own works in this way).

128

Philosophy

Schlemmer's philosophical expositions include a history of philosophy, a history of the origin of life and of man (in part natural
philosophy), definitions of the concepts 'biology', 'psychology'
and 'philosophy', and an explanation of the concept 'substance'.
The concepts 'philosophy' and 'substance' were treated from the
point of view of the history of philosophy.
The tabular survey of the history of philosophy here reproduced is
followed in the notes by a more detailed presentation of the
several philosophical theories and schools.

Bibliography to the chapter on philosophy
[After O. Schlemmer]

Boetius, AMTS, *die Tröstungen der Philosophie*. Leipzig 1893. [*De consolatione philosophiae*].

Bruno, Giordano, *Von der Ursache, dem Prinzip und dem Einen*. Leipzig 1909. [*De la causa, principio ed uno*].

Descartes, René, *Abhandlungen über die Methode des richtigen Vernunftgebrauches und der wissenschaftlichen Wahrheitsforschung*. Leipzig 1925. [*Discours de la méthode*].

Eucken, Rudolf, *Geistesprobleme und Lebensfragen*. Leipzig 1918.

Fichte, Johann G., *Die Bestimmung des Menschen*. Leipzig 1897.

Grau, Kurt, *Grundriss der Logik*. Leipzig-Berlin 1918.

Hamann, Johann Georg, *Hamanns Magie und Sokratische Denkwürdigkeiten*. Leipzig 1877.

Herbertz, Richard, *Die Philosophie des Raumes*. Stuttgart 1912.

Hume, David, *Eine Untersuchung über den menschlichen Verstand*. Leipzig 1912. [*An enquiry concerning human understanding*].

Kant, Immanuel, *Grundlegung zur Metaphysik der Sitten*. Leipzig 1906.

Leibniz, Gottfried Wilhelm, *Kleinere philosophische Schriften*. Leipzig 1900.

Locke, John, *Über den menschlichen Verstand*. Leipzig 1918. [*An essay concerning human understanding*].

Pascal, Blaise, *Blaise Pascals Gedanken*. Leipzig 1918. [*Pensées*].

Schwegler, Friedrich Karl Albert, *Geschichte der Philosophie im Umriss*. Leipzig 1889.

Spengler, Oswald, *Untergang des Abendlandes*. Munich 1918. [*The Decline of the West*].

Voltaire, François Marie (no title).

Ziegler, Ernst, *Kants Sittenlehre in gemeinverständlicher Darstellung*. Leipzig 1919.

19.10.28

Tabular surveys of the history of philosophy and the main schools of thought
(after Wilh. Wundt)

I. Philosophy of the Greeks

1. Period of cosmological speculation

   Idea of the unity of the world

   Macrocosmic idea:
   Unity of the substance of the world:
   Earlier Ionic natural philosophers
   Thales – Anaximander – Anaximenes

   Unity of the world order
   Quantitative principle: Qualitative principle:
   Pythagoreans
   (Conformity to mathe-   Continuous   Natural
   matical laws)   being   change
                                  Eleatics   Heraclitus

   Microcosmic idea:
   Idea of ordered substance (theory of elements)
   Quantitative: Qualitative:
   Atomistic   Later Ionic natural
   Leucippus, Democritus   philosophers
                                  (Empedocles, Anaxagoras)

- -

2. Period of the universal systems of science

   Preliminary period:

   Ethical problem

   Negative ethical schools of thought:

   Point of view of individual expediency   Sceptical empiricism

   Sophistry

   Positive ethical schools of thought:

   Point of view of universal expediency, concept of universal knowledge

   Problem of self-knowledge

   Socrates

   Period of the great systems:
   Universal direction of philosophy
   Problem of knowledge of self and of the world
   Opposition of the ideal and real world
   First idealistic system

   Plato

   Academic School

t a b e l l a r i s c h e   u e b e r s i c h t e n   zur

g e s c h i c h t e   d e r   p h i l o s o f i e   und ihrer

h a u p t r i c h t u n g e m   (nach wilh.w.u.n.d.t.)....

I. P H I L O S O F I E   D E R   G R I E C H E N

1. p e r i o d e   der   k o s m o l o g i s c h e n
s p e k u l a t i o n .

i d e e   d e r   w e l t e i n h e i t
makrokosmische idee

e i n h e i t   des   w e l t s t o f f s :
aeltere jonische physiker
thales- anaximander- anaximenes
248   17   17

e i n h e i t   d e r   w e l t o r d n u n g
q u a n t i t a t i v e s   prinzip: /q u a l i t a t i v e s   pr.
pythagoreer 206
(mathematische gesetzmaessig-   beharrendes   gesetzmaessige
keit)   sein   veraenderung
eleaten 65   heraklit 117

m i k r o k o s m i s c h e   i d e e :
i d e e   des   g e o r d n e t e n   s t o f f s (elementen-
lehre)
q u a n t i t a t i v e :   q u a l i t a t i v e :
atomistik   juengere jonische physiker
(leukipp,demokrit)52   (empedokles.anaxagoras)
69   76

2. p e r i o d e   d e r   u n i v e r s e l l e n   w i s s e n s —
s c h a f t s s y s t e m e

v o r p e r i o d e :   Ethik wö ?81
e t h i s c h e s   p r o b l e m
I
negativ-ethische richtungen:
individueller nuetzlichkeits-   skeptischer empirismus
standpunkt
s o p h i s t i k 236
I
positiv-ethische richtungen:
universeller nuetzlichkeitsstandpunkt,begriff des allgemeingueltige
wissens. problem der selbsterkenntnis
s o k r a t e s 235
I
p e r i o d e   d e r   g r o s s e n   s y s t e m e :
universelle richtung der philosofie
problem der selbst-und welterkenntnis
gegensatz der idealen und realen welt
erstes idealistisches system
p l a t o 197
akademische schule
I

hinauf:

einheit der idealen und realen welt
erstes realistisches system
a r i s t o t e l e s 25
peripatische schule (*genannt nach der Oängen des Lykeion (Peripatoi*
in dem A. zu lehren pflegte)

----

3. z e i t a l t e r   d e s   h e l l e n i s m u s
(ethisch-theologische periode)
p r i n z i p   d e r   s e l b s t v e r v o l l k o m m nung
(individualismus - kosmopolitismus - monismus)

rigorismus: x 217 wö   skeptizismus: 234   eudaemonismus: 82
stoizismus x 242 "   phyrrhonismus x   epikureimus   76
      akademiker 77   peripatetiker 10.

I

p r i n z i p   d e r   r e l i g i o e s e n   e r h e b u n g
(emanationssysteme(a)religioese mystik und mantik)(*hafologoturm*)
neupythagoreer. juedische theosophen 250 ,neuplatoniker

I

u e b e r g a n g   d e r   p h i l o s o f i e   in
t h e o s o f i e 250

NNNNN==

II/C H R I S T L I C H E   P H I L O S O F I E

1. p a t r i s t i s c h e   p h i l o s o f i e : (*Der kirchenväter, welche*
die christl. Dogmatik mit
der antiken philos. verknüpft

f e s t s t e l l u n g   der glaubensdogmen

emanationssysteme	orthodoxe lehre	rationalistische systeme
phantastische mystik	r e i n e	verstandesmaessige auffassg
I	m y s t i k : 145	I
neuplatonismus	kosmologisches	aristotelische philosofie
(gnostizismus) 102	problem	(monarchismus)
	(irenaeus)	
	I	
	theologisches problem (*J. Lehre von Gott*) 105	
	(athanasius)	
	I	
	ethisches problem	
	(augustin)	

2. s c h o l a s t i s c h e   p h i l o s o f i e : 223
beweis der glaubensdogmen

t r a n s z e n d e n t e r 253 r e a l i s m u s
(universalia ante rem)
begruendung der ontologie 187
(anselmus von canterbury , wilhelm von champeaux)
scholastik des 11.und 12. jahrhunderts.

I

i m m a n e n t e r 149 r e a l i s m u s
(universalia in re)
aristotelische scholastik
(albertus magnus , thomas von aquino , duns scotus)
scholastik des 13.jahrhunderts

I

n o m i n a l i s m u s V.2.ff.
(universalia post rem)
trennung von glauben und wissen
(wilhelm von occam)
scholastik des 14.jahrhunderts

Unity of the ideal and real world
First realist system

Aristotle

Peripatetic School

- -

3. Hellenistic age

(Ethical, theological period)

Principle of self-perfection
(individualism – cosmopolitanism – monism)

Rigorism	Scepticism	Eudaemonism
Stoicism	Pyrrhonism	Epicureanism
Academics	Peripatetics	

Principle of religious exaltation

(systems of emanation, religious mysticism and divination)

Neo-Pythagoreans. Jewish theosophists, Neo-Platonists

Transition from philosophy to theosophy

II. Christian philosophy

1. Patristic philosophy :

Identification of the dogmas of belief

Systems of emanation	Orthodox theory	Rationalist systems
Fantastic mysticism	Pure mysticism :	Rational interpretation
Neo-Platonism	Cosmological	Aristotelian philosophy
(Gnosticism)	problem	(Monarchism)
	(Irenaeus)	
	Theological problem	
	(Athanasius)	
	Ethical problem	
	(Augustine)	

2. Scholastic philosophy :

Proof of the dogmas of faith

Transcendental realism
(universalia ante rem)
Establishment of ontology
(Anselm of Canterbury, William of Champeaux)
Scholasticism of the 11th and 12th centuries

Immanent realism
(universalia in re)
Aristotelian scholasticism
(Albertus Magnus, Thomas Aquinas, Duns Scotus)
Scholasticism of the 13th century

Nominalism
(universalia post rem)
Separation of faith and knowledge
(William of Ockham)
Scholasticism of the 14th century

III. Later philosophy

1. Age of the emancipation of thought

    a. Idea of eternity:
Eternity of the world. End of the imperfection of the individual, God an eternal higher order:
Idea of absolute eternity
(Nicholas of Cusa)

    b. Idea of the analogy of all beings and of evolution
Man a microcosm
(Paracelsus)

    c. Idea of the independence of the individual existence and of its structure
Concept of the monad. God the monas monadum
(Giordano Bruno)

- -

2. Age of conflicting philosophies of life

Inductive, empirical		Deductive, speculative
	school	
Bacon		
Naturalistic		Theological
	modes of thought	
Hobbes		Geulincx
Gassendi		Malebranche
Materialism	Mysticism and scepticism (Pascal. Bayle)	Spiritualism

- -

3. Age of the dogmatic systems

Rationalism   Empiricism
Theory of naturalistic perception (Locke)

Realism	Idealism		
Universalism	Individualism		
Pantheism	Theism		
(Spinoza)	(Leibniz)		
		Subjectivism	Objectivism
		Idealism	Materialism
		(Berkeley)	(English and French free-thinkers)
Critical, sceptical	Dogmatic		Philosophy of feeling
Empiricism	Eclecticism		Rousseau, Hamann etc.
(Hume)	(Wolff and his school)		

- -

4. Age of modern philosophy

Kant's critical philosophy
Idealistic   Realistic
schools

3

III₂ N E U E R E   P H I L O S O F I E

1. z e i t a l t e r   der   b e f r e i u n g   des   d e n k e n s

a. i d e e   der   u n e n d l i c h k e i t:
unendlichkeit der welt.aufhebung der unvollkommenheit des ein-
zelnen, gott ein unendliches hoeherer ordnung :
idee der absoluten unendlichkeit
(nikolaus von cues)

b. i d e e   der   a n a l o g i e   a l l e r   w e s e n
und   der   e n t w i c k l u n g
der mensch ein mikrokosmus
(paracelsus)

c. i d e e   der   s e l b s t s t a e n d i g k e i
der   e i n z e l w e s e n   und ihrer   s t u f e n —
o r d n u n g
der begriff der monade.gott die monas monadum
(giordano bruno) 45

2. z e i t a l t e r   des   K a m p f e s   der   w e l t -
a n s c h a u u n g e n

induktiv-empirische 130   deduktiv-spekulative 51
I   richtung   I
bacon
n a t u r a l i s t i s c h e | t h e o l o g i s c h e
I   d e n k w e i s e n   I
hobbes   geulinx
gassendi   malebranche
I   I
materialismus   mystizismus   spiritualismus 140
und skeptizismus
(pascal. bayle)

3. z e i t a l t e r   der   d o g m a t i s c h e n   s y t e m e 61

r a t i o n a l i s m u s 207   e m p i r i s m u s

realismus 210 | idealismus 125   naturalistische erkennt-
255 universalismus individualismus 137   nislehre (locke) 157
189 phanteismus theismus 249
(spinoza) 239   (leibniz)   subjektivismus- objektivismus 185
155   idealismus 243 materialismus
(berkeley)   (engl.u.franz.
freidenker
kritisch-skeptischer   dogmatischer   gefuehlsphilosofie
empirismus   ekklektizismus 68 rousseau.hamann etc.
(hume) 122   (wolff u.seine schule) 212

4. z e i t a l t e r   der   n e u e s t e n   p h i l o s o f i e

kants kritische philosofie.

i d e a l i s t i s c h e   r e a l i s t i s c h e
r i c h t u n g e n

(verwebt nächste Seite)

4. z e i t a l t e r d e r n e u e s t e n p h i l o s o f i e

kants[135] kritische philosofie

i d e a l i s t i s c h e   xxxxxxxixixxxixxxxxxx
r i c h t u n g e n

primat d.prakt.[201]   parallele entw.   primat d.theoret.
vernunft   von natur   vernunft
i d e a l i s t .   und geist   i d e a l i s t i s c h e
s t a a t s -u n d   p a n t h e i s t.   g e s c h i c h t s p h i l o s o f i e
e r z i e h u n g s-   n a t u r p h.
l e h r e
fichte 86   schelling 218   hegel 115

r e a l i s t i s c h e r i c h t u n g :

i n d i v i d u a l i s m u s | universaliam. | positivismus 109
(monadolgie | |
herbart 118 | (willensmetaph| einfluss der
                             | physik) | positiven wissen-
                             | schopenhauer | schaften
                             | 225 |

xxxxxxxxxxxxxxxxxxxxxxxxxxxxxxxxxxxxxxxxxxxxxxxxxxxxxxxxxxxxxxxxxxxxx

H A U P T R I C H T U N G E N D E R P H I L O S O F I E

I. e r k e n n t n i s t h e o r e t i s c h e r i c h t u n g e n 78-79

e m p i r i s m.[72] r a t i o n a l i s m.[210] k r i t i z i s m.[148]
naiver   apriorismus 23   negativer -positiver
reflektierender   ontologismus 187   skeptizism. eigentl.
reiner   panlogismus 789   kritizism.

II. m e t a p h y s i s c h e r i c h t u n g e n 169

1. m a t e r i a l i s m u s 163
dualistischer............monistischer
(demokrit,gassendi)
                    mechanistischer---psychophysischer
                         (hobbes)   (toland,diderot) 58
                          120   I
                      psychologischer- soziologischer
                                          (marx.engels
                      lokalisation
                      komlexer funktionen 159 das bewusstsein
                      (phrenologie)   ein summationsphaeno-
                                                  men
                                           (materialistische
                                             psycholgie)

2. i d e a l i s m u s
o b j e k t i v e r | s u b j e k t i v e r | t r a n s z e n d e n-
                    | | t a l e r

dualist. monisti.   (kant) 135
(plato) 197 (leibniz) 155   (berkeley) 39   I
augustin   idealrealismus
(uebergangsstufe   subjektiver-objekt.-absoluter
                                  fichte   schelling   hegel
                                    86   218   115

3.

4. Age of modern philosophy

Kant's critical philosophy

Idealistic school:

Primacy of practical reason Idealistic political and educational theory Fichte	Parallel development of nature and mind Pantheistic natural philosophy Schelling	Primacy of theoretical reason Idealistic philosophy of history Hegel

Realistic school:

Individualism Monadology Herbart	Universalism (Metaphysics of the will) Schopenhauer	Positivism Influence of the positive sciences

---

Main schools of philosophy

I. Epistemological schools

Empiricism	Rationalism	Critical philosophy	
simple	a-priorism	negative	positive
reflective	ontologism	scepticism	true critical
pure	panlogism		philosophy

- -

II. Metaphysical schools

        1. Materialism

dualistic . . . . monistic
(Democritus, Gassendi)

      mechanistic — psychophysical
      (Hobbes)   (Toland, Diderot)

          psychological — sociological
                          (Marx. Engels)

localization of complex functions (phrenology)	the consciousness a phenomenon of summation (materialist psychology)

        2. Idealism

Objective		Subjective	Transcendental
Dualist	Monist		
(Plato)	(Leibniz)	(Berkeley)	(Kant)
St Augustine (transitional phase)			Ideal realism

Subjective — Objective — Absolute
Fichte   Schelling   Hegel

3. Realism

Dualistic
of principles – of substances
(Aristotle)   (Descartes)

Monistic
transcendental – immanent
(Spinoza)   individual – universal
                                    (Herbart)   (Schopenhauer)

- -

III. Ethical schools (systems of morality)

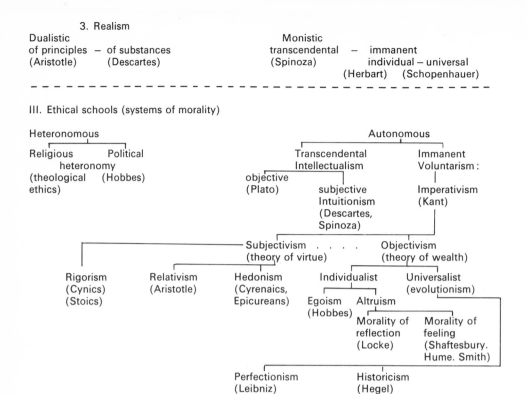

Heteronomous

Autonomous

Religious   Political
        heteronomy
(theological   (Hobbes)
ethics)

Transcendental   Immanent
Intellectualism   Voluntarism:

objective
(Plato)

subjective
Intuitionism
(Descartes,
Spinoza)

Imperativism
(Kant)

Subjectivism . . . .   Objectivism
(theory of virtue)   (theory of wealth)

Rigorism   Relativism   Hedonism   Individualist   Universalist
(Cynics)   (Aristotle)   (Cyrenaics,   (evolutionism)
(Stoics)   Epicureans)

Egoism   Altruism
(Hobbes)

Morality of   Morality of
reflection   feeling
(Locke)   (Shaftesbury.
                     Hume. Smith)

Perfectionism   Historicism
(Leibniz)   (Hegel)

        3. r e a l i s m u s   m o n i s t i s c h e r
 d u a l i s t i s c h e r
 der prinzipien - der substanzen   transzendenter- immanenter 129
   (aristoteles) (descartes)   (spinoza) individuals-
        25   54   239   universal.
                                                      (herbart)
                                                       (schopenhauer
                                                              225

- -
 III. e t h i s c h e 87 r i c h t u n g e n (m o r a l s y s t e m e)

 h e t e r o n o m e 36   a u t o n o m e 36
            I   I
 religioese/politische   transzendente   immanente
        heteronomie   I   I
 (theol.   (hobbes)   intellektualigm. /voluntarism:
 ethik)   135   imperativismus 129
                               objektiver/subjektiver (kant)
                               (plato) intuitionismus 136
                                        (descartes,
                                         spinoza)

      subjektivismus............objektivismus
      (tugendlehre)254   (gueterlehre)109
            I   I
 217 rigorism.-relativism.-hedonism.   individualist./universalist.
 151(kyniker) (stoiker) (kyrenaiker,   I   (evolutionism.)93
 (stoiker) (aristoteles)epikureer)   64egoism./altruism.74
        242   (hobbes)   I
                                     212reflexionsmoral/gefueh
                                     (locke)   moral
                                              (shaftesbu
                                              hume.smith)
                                                122

           perfektionism. / historism. 120
           (leibniz)   (hegel)
              155   115

Third day (27/4/28)

History of the origins of (1) life
                                      (2) man
(parallel to the 'simple forms and measurements of man').

First:

Point and purpose of **science**: to assemble and classify what can be known: in contrast to speculative **philosophy** and in complete contrast to **religion** and **art**, which **invent**.
Basic limitation of human knowledge in relation to the dimensions of the world: it always gives the image and concept of the world as they exist in the human brain, but never the world itself.
Aim of science: mathematical formula of the mechanical events of the world.
In this sense **Pythagoras** claimed that number was the basis of all study of the world.
Leonardo da Vinci: 'no human experience can be called true science until it has been submitted to mathematical proof'.
Galileo: 'nature is written in the language of mathematics'.
Kant: 'I believe that each particular theory of nature contains only so much of true science as it contains of mathematics'.
Schopenhauer: 'the aim and ideal of all natural science is a thoroughgoing materialism'.
Helmholtz said that the final goal of all science was to become resolved into mechanics.
Dubois-Reymond: 'for the natural scientist there is no knowledge other than mechanical knowledge, wretched substitute for true knowledge though it may be!'
The course of the world is mechanistic – (individuality = structure of atoms; personality = universal course of the albumen molecule) but the world itself need not be. It is unknowable.
The following questions remain unsolved (by science): What is the world? Why is it? For what? Whence? Whither? Is there a creator, immortality, retribution, predestination? Is the knowable world all that exists? Is the existence that is revealed to us as world and experience real at all or is it perhaps only the dream of a dreaming self? Etc. . . .
Hence
The wisdom of the natural scientists in their old age:
Newton: 'I see myself as a boy who here and there on the shore of knowledge has picked up a coloured shell',
Goethe: 'we all walk in mystery'
Dubois-Reymond (the mechanistic natural scientist!): 'we do not know, we shall not know!'

Within science the **conflict** of the savants:
mainly concerning
Dualism and **Monism**

	Theism	(God as a personality	Pantheism (God is nature)			
	immaterial	similar to the	God	mind	energy	
Dualism:	**God**	human)	and	and	and	Monism
	material		nature	body	material	
	world					

Psychology

Almost the only documentary evidence of Oskar Schlemmer's lectures on psychology are the syllabuses. Only these and the bibliography throw any light on the contents of these lectures. Psychological and philosophical observations often overlap, especially in his presentation of the concept of substance, which is derived from philosophical and psychological schools of thought.

Bibliography to the chapter on psychology
[After O. Schlemmer]

Aster, Ernst von, *Einführung in die Psychologie*. Leipzig and Berlin 1922.

Carus, Carl Gustav, *Psyche*. 1864.

Carus, Carl Gustav, *Symbolik der menschlichen Gestalt*. Celle 1925.

Erismann, Theodor, *Psychologie*. Leipzig and Berlin 1920/21.

Federn-Meng, *Das psychoanalytische Volksbuch*. Stuttgart 1926.

Giese, Fritz, *Psychologisches Wörterbuch*. Leipzig 1928.

Klages, Ludwig, *Ausdrucksbewegung und Gestaltungskraft*. Leipzig 1923.

Klages, Ludwig, *Mensch und Erde*. Munich 1920.

Klages, Ludwig, *Vom kosmogonischen Eros*. Jena 1922.

Klages, Ludwig, *Vom Wesen des Bewusstseins*. Leipzig 1926.

Perty, Maximilian, *Die mystischen Erscheinungen der menschlichen Natur*. 1861.

Trömmer, Ernst, *Hypnotismus und Suggestion*. Leipzig and Berlin 1922.

Wenzel, Alois, *Das unbewusste Denken*. Karlsruhe 1927.

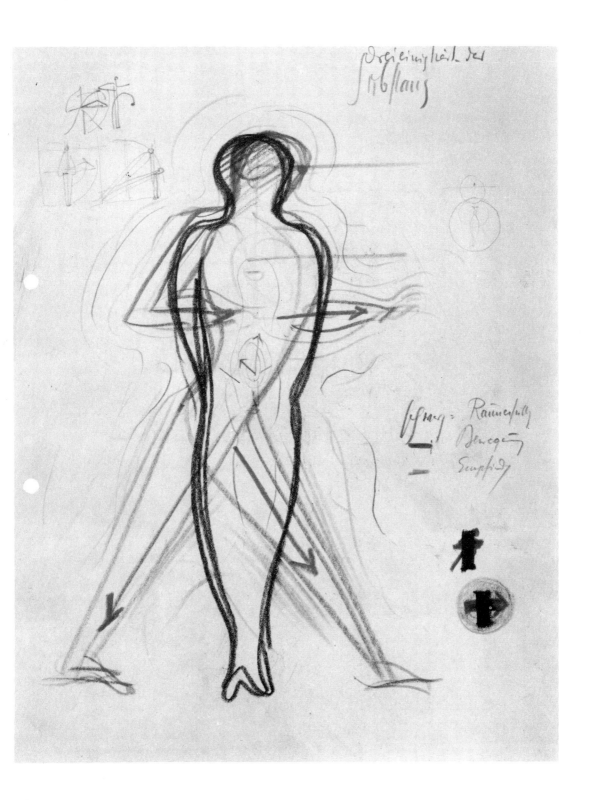

145

13.9.28
Psychology (psychics)
Heraclitus: 'You will not find
the frontiers of the soul
though you scour every street,
so deep is its ground.'

2 courses for treating experience: one is **natural science**: it examines the
object of the experience in its character of supposed independence of the
subject. The other is **psychology**: it examines the total content of the experience in its relations with the **subject** and in the qualities directly attached to
it. Old concepts: 'science of the soul', 'science of the inner experience', 'self-
knowledge of the subject'.

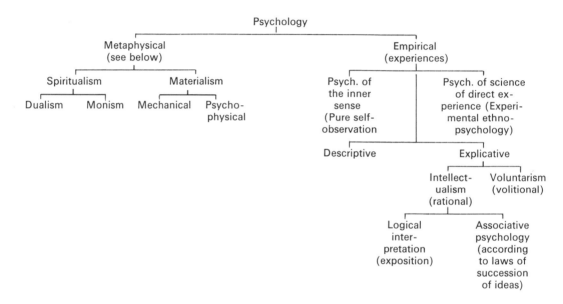

Metaphysical psychology seeks to discover a definition of the '**nature of
the soul**'.
Spiritualist psychology sees psychic events as the workings of a **specific**
substance of the psyche, which is either regarded as essentially different from
matter or as related to it in essence. (Dualist psychology, Monist psychology)

13.9.28.

Psychologie (Seelenlehre)

Heraklit: "der Seele Grenzen
kannst du nicht ausfinden,
und ob du jeglichen Weg
abschrittest: so tiefen Grund
hat sie."

2 Richtungen für die Bearbeitung der Erfahrung: die eine ist die Naturwissenschaft:
sie betrachtet die Objekte der Erfahrung in ihrer vom dem Subjekt unabhängig
gedachten Beschaffenheit.   Die andere ist die der Psychologie:
sie untersucht den gesamten Inhalt der Erfahrung in seinen Beziehungen
zum Subjekt u. den ihm von diesem unmittelbar beigelegten Eigenschaften.
alte Begriffe: "Wissenschaft von der Seele"; "Wissenschaft der inneren Erfahrung";
"Selbsterkenntnis des Subjekts".

Metaphysische   Psychologie   Empirische
  (s.d.)   (erfahrungs-)

Spiritualismus   Materialismus   Ps. d. inneren   Ps. als Wissenschaft
                                             Sinnes   d. unmittelbaren
Dualismus   Monismus   Mechanischer Psychophysischer (Reine Seelen-   Erfahrung (Experimental-
                                                        kunde)   u. Völkerpsychologie)

                                      Deskriptive   Explikative
                                      (beschreibende)   (auslegende)

                                      Intellektualismus   Voluntarismus
                                      (verstandesmäßig)   (willensmäßig)

                                  Logik   Assoziations-
                                  Interpretation   psychologie
                                  (Auslegung)   (und Gesetze d. Aufeinanderfolge
                                                           u. Verkettungen)

Die Metaphys. Ps.   sucht eine Begriffsbestimmung vom "Wesen der Seele" zu gewinnen.
Die Spiritualist. Ps. betrachtet die psychischen Vorgänge als die Wirkungen einer spezifischen
Dualistische P.   Seelensubstanz, die je nachdem wesentlich verschieden von der Materie
monist. P.   oder als ihr wesensverwandt
                       angesehen wird.

Questions and answers to the preliminary course 'man'

Questions on 18.5.28

(1) Which part of the course do you like best? The biological part or figure drawing?

(2) What subject (in the chapter 'man') interests you particularly?

(3) Would you like the subjects to be treated more briefly or in greater detail?

(4) Do you decide for Monism or Dualism? For Mechanism or Vitalism? For Theism or Pantheism?

(5) Why are you doing no work?

Outcome of the answers

		?	Lux F.	Fern-bach	Comer.	Leutho	Hassen Marx	O Berger Mey Wa Lo Burk
For biology								
Against biology								
For figure drawing								
Against figure drawing								
For philosophy								
Against philosophy								
Special wishes				space		space art dance theory of colours	stage	
					discuss	short presenta-tion of the essentials first, then discussion		question: free work or in light of the given subjects: both.

----

1) welchen teil des unterrichts bevorzugen Sie? den biologischen oder
   den des figurenzeichnens?

2) welches stoffgebiet (bei dem kapitel "mensch") interessiert Sie besonders?

3) wünschen Sie die themen kürzer oder ausführlicher behandelt?

4) entscheiden Sie sich für monismus oder dualismus? für mechanismus oder
   vitalismus? für theismus oder pantheismus?

5) warum arbeiten Sie nichts?

Outcome of the answers

			?	lux f.	fernbach	comer.	leutho	hassen marx	o berger mey wa lo burk
für biologisch			———	———					
gegen "					———				
für figurzeich					———	———			———
gegen "									
für filosof.						———			
gegen "									
besondere wünsche				r aum			raum kunst tanz farbl· bühne		

Written answers to the questions [of 18.5.1928] [1]

[1] The answers are mostly written in lower-case letters.

I prefer the <u>biological</u> teaching.

I prefer the 'biological part' of the teaching.

Lux Feininger

I am mainly interested in the art and drawing part because I know the biological things from school and from books. Since time is so very limited I earnestly ask that they should be shortened to make way for the <u>spatial problems</u> which are so temptingly announced in the syllabus, with reference to man in general. We have had a systematic course on <u>plane</u> with Klee, to our joy the word 'space' was also in Moholy's syllabus for the last II semester, but the concept was hardly mentioned. It is a great lack that in none of the art teaching is anything said about space ; perhaps it would be possible within the framework of this course, eventually to extend drawing from the nude to include 'man in space'.

Eva Fernbach

1. Figural, but without neglecting the biological.
2. I am most interested in the subject of a <u>philosophy of life</u>, this is the <u>paramount question</u> today and, as regards the official sylla-bus, is totally neglected at the Bauhaus.
3. Non-essentials briefly, important subjects (see above) fully (with discussion).
4. Monism (and Mechanism).
5. Because I have already done most of the figure drawing last term.

Erich Comeriner

The subjects which interest me most are : man and space, dance, man and art, the psyche, philosophy, theory of colours.
I think the subject of anatomy could be shortened as most people probably know it already.
I find the subjects of the whole syllabus interesting. I should find it excellent if the master could explain the whole thing to us first and then start a discussion, or even an exchange of opinion from our side. Although I have not done any work yet, I have made several starts but have come to grief on things about which I was not clear. In fact, I am in the dark about many things connected with measurement and the theory of proportion.

Leuthold

1. Figure drawing

2. Mechanics of the body, movement, static and kinetic impulses. Inclusion of the subject : man and stage (diagrams of movement), mechanics of the stage.

3. As hitherto (in figure drawing).

4. (a) The explanations of the concepts which we have been given are insufficient to enable one to decide.

(b) The question is too individual and has too many other connotations to be dealt with during figure drawing.

5. I work 1. for the workshop (practical) – 2. for the workshop (theoretical) – 3. (a) statics ; (b) figure drawing.

If I have not done enough work on figure drawing this is simply a question of time and not a question of interest.

Hassenpflug, Marx

1. Figure drawing in the light of biological functions.

2. The human body.

3. Objective treatment of the subjects.

4.   ?

5. We do not see what the idea is, free artistic creation or set work following the given scheme. We find no incitement to work freely.

Otti Berger, Wera Mayer-Waldeck, Lo Burk[hardt]

Dear Herr Schlemmer,   Dessau, 1.6.1928

In the following note I will try to explain my position with regard to your course.

The set general subject 'man' from the biological, anatomical and psychological angle is so vast a field that several semesters could be devoted to each section ; the subject warrants it and it would be the one way of providing a thorough education.

The work in the first term (Kandinsky) begins with an examination of the starting points of the formal elements, of forms and their coloration. In the second term (Klee) forms are examined from the angle of their internal coherence, up to the point of primary figuration. All this two-dimensionally only. Thus there is no examination of plastic form. I think it would be a very good thing if discussion of this subject were to provide the material for our course, with man as the final result, from the purely artistic point of view. Further development, man in space, the stage.

What I have said above also gives you part of the reason why I do not work. For the rest, I find it impossible to make analytical studies which represent no problem to me.

I write this as a rough outline of my view.

Yours, Lo Lang

Postscript

Oskar Schlemmer's figuration

'I must admit that I feel myself more and more drawn to philosophy, to the analytical approach, and paint almost unwillingly. It is perhaps the feeling that many things are brewing . . .[1] An analytical approach – in thought but also in his artistic works – usually comes to an artist when he is in an unclear situation or in a process of fermentation and needs to clarify his ideas. Schlemmer saw himself faced with disparate artistic expressional means and was unable to come down on one side or the other, for he saw possibilities for himself on both hands. Long before the Bauhaus period he had stood between Cubist and abstract painting on the one hand and Expressionism on the other. Both sides offered him useful material and it was therefore a matter of resolving the – presumably only apparent – conflict between these possibilities. As an entry in his diary and, particularly his work, show, Schlemmer saw painting as a metaphor: 'Representation of man will always form the great metaphor for the artist.'[2] This interpretation obliged him not to abandon the 'object', but he saw that the unambiguousness of the abstract means contains a power which cannot be forfeited if the artistic message is to make its full impact. For Schlemmer this situation gave rise to the question of how a metaphorical pictorial form for man and the world can be achieved with abstract means. If line, plane, chiaroscuro and colour can be applied from two different angles – to objectivize an 'abstract' pictorial idea or to objectivize an imaginative impulse which shapes a 'representational' image – the geometrical figures too, which are formed from these means, can be applied from two angles, the abstract and the representational. Having regard to his intentions, Schlemmer decided in favour of the second angle. Line and plane were used in the form of geometrical figures; but Schlemmer did not go the way of analytical Cubism, he did not

[1] Oskar Schlemmer, Diary, 30 April 1919.

[2] Oskar Schlemmer, Diary, November 1919.

152

move towards making the geometric figures autonomous and eliminating the static or dynamic structure of the image; he turned instead in the opposite direction: the geometrical figure became an element in a compact, pictorial human figure — Schlemmer stood in the tradition of Marées and Seurat — and the geometrical elements gave the image an architectonically constructive framework. Geometric figuration yielded a formula for the human shape.

The formula — the most concise schema evoked by an objective association — served as a footing for the leap from the representation of nature to the artistic objectivization of a pictorial idea. Schlemmer needed to analyze in order to discover this formula. His analysis consisted of being able to represent parts of the human body or the whole body and its pictorial environment in shortened form with a restricted number of geometrical elements — such as dot, circle, curve and straight line. In this way Schlemmer evolved an 'objective' formal scheme which could be developed into a differentiated formal vocabulary. Thus he moved from a graphic, two-dimensional pictorial concept to a spatial one and in the process the form became more complex and more diversely stratified. In the end — particularly in his 'window pictures' — Schlemmer achieved that high level of intellectual reality which belongs to a form in which a proper balance is struck between geometric schema, visual observation and expression.

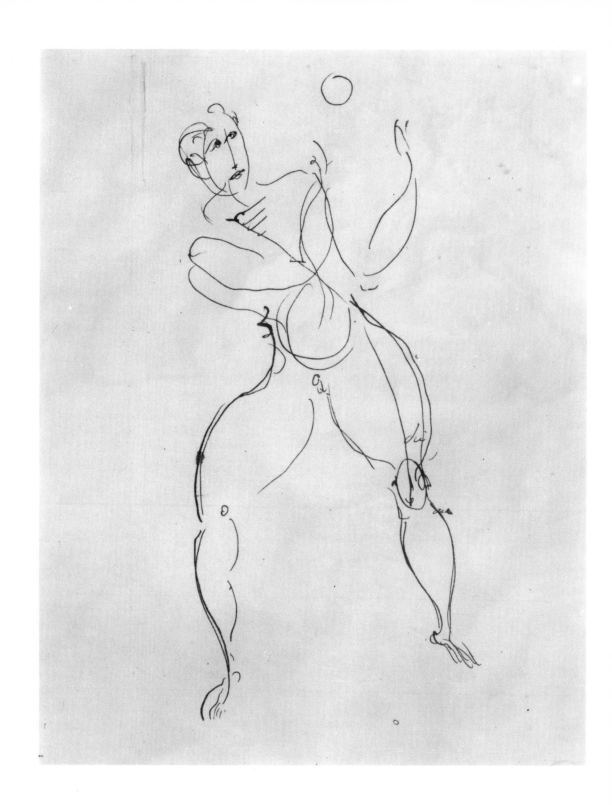

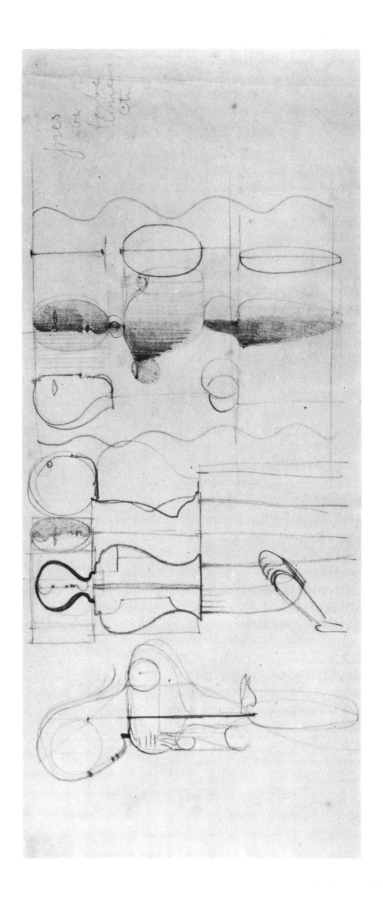

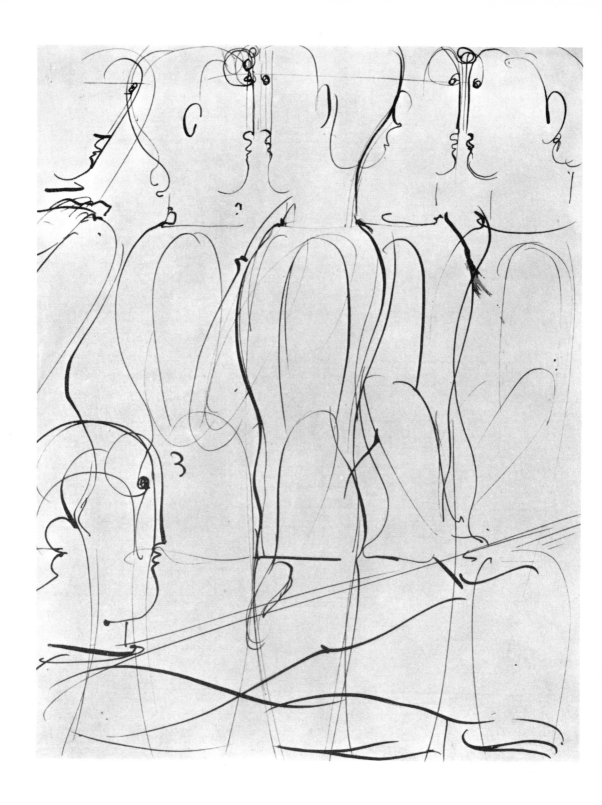

159